PLANNING FOR METROPOLITAN CITIES
A Suggestive Approach

PLANNING FOR METROPOLITAN CITIES
A Suggestive Approach

M. PRATAP RAO

CONCEPT PUBLISHING COMPANY, NEW DELHI - 110059

ISBN 81-7022-306-7

First Published 1990

Published by
Ashok Kumar Mittal
Concept Publishing Company
A/15-16, Commercial Block, Mohan Garden
NEW DELHI-110059 (India)

Lasertypeset by
Microtech Advance Printing Systems (Pvt.) Ltd.
H-13, Bali Nagar
NEW DELHI - 10015

Printed in India by
Taj Press
DELHI - 110 006

CONTENTS

LIST OF MAPS

LIST OF GRAPHS

LIST OF TABLES

PREFACE

A COMPREHENSIVE view of the book is given below :

Identified Problem

The increasing growth and number of metropolitan cities in the country is a cause of concern for the past few decades. There are 12 metropolitan cities in India as per 1981 Census. The problems due to rapid growth of these cities are well known.

Solutions in Practice

There are several measures taken by various metropolitan authorities depending on the nature of their problems. One of the widely used measures to de-centralise the growth is the development of satellite towns, ring towns, new towns, etc. The experiments are found to be successful at some places and not so in some other places.

Drawbacks in the Present Approach

The development plans of the metropolitan cities lay emphasis on land-use. The new towns developed as satellite towns or ring towns are guided by the zonal development plans; which are basically land-use plans. At this juncture, it is pertinent to bring out two important issues on which this book tries to elucidate :

(a) An unending debate is going on, on what should be a satellite town, ring town, new town, etc., particularly about their definition, location and content. In these heated arguments, the essential purpose of organising the inevitable growth of metropolitan cities is lost. It should be accepted that a city cannot grow extremely mono-centric. There should be sub-centres to de-centralise the growth. This should form the crux of the problem and the book tries to highlight this angle. It does not debate on what a ring town should be or its definition. It tries to interpret how best its purpose derived from the development plan could be achieved.

(b) There is an increasing emphasis on detailed land-use planning in our zonal development plans and also in the development plans in general. This book tries to focus that a basic structure plan of the area is important before working the land-use details.

Suggested Approach

Having accepted the fact that it is essential to develop sub-centres around the main centre of the metropolis, it is necessary to identify the potential work and service centres around whom the increasing growth could be de-centralised. After identifying these areas, it is necessary to find out the function, commercial core, hierarchy of shopping centres, road network, industrial sites, employment potential, etc., of the area. Based on these factors a 'Structure Plan' should be prepared containing the future development policies in the area. These aspects are substantiated with the help of a case study.

The basic framework for this approach has been derived from the development plan system adopted in the Town and Country Planning Act, 1971 of Great Britain.

Acknowledgements

I thank the then faculty members of urban and regional planning department, Institute of Development Studies, University of Mysore, Mysore, Mr. P.D. Mahadev, Mr. R.N. Achyutha, Mr. B.S. Bhoosan and Mr. N.N. Sastry for their inspiration and timely guidance in shaping the work.

I invite any criticism on the book because the essential purpose of the book is to provoke new thinking on the subject rather than give a universal solution.

M. PRATAP RAO

1

INTRODUCTION

CITY IS the reflection of the civilisation. The origin, growth and decay of a city is as natural as any civilisation. There is no need to lament and cry in anguish at the growing deterioration of the environment in the cities as long as scientific knowledge is in hand. Order becomes meaningless when there is no disorder, organisation has no purpose where there is no disorganisation and improvement is a loose-talk when there is no deterioration. Change, whether good or bad, is necessary for human existence and city is no exception. Every change need not lead to betterment because change will lose its importance of innovation and novelty if it is made precise. In this kind of constantly changing environment, what all human beings need is The Awareness and make the senses work than to live in resignation or revolt.

Urbanisation is a phenomenon experienced everywhere in the world at a faster rate after the industrial revolution. City became a centre of industrialisation. When a city grows it adds new population and migration is an important feature for the fast growth of cities. The urban growth in India is high for the past three decades. The pressure on the metropolitan cities in view of the migration particularly from the smaller towns for employment has created several problems regarding its expansion and organisation to meet the growing needs.

Different strategies have been evolved in guiding and organising the metropolitan growth. One such strategy is the development of new towns or expanded towns as satellite or ring towns within the metropolitan region. The major drawback in this strategy is the lack of continuity of urban and rural planning.

The metropolitan planning is still an isolated planning exercise in India. The new towns or expanded towns proposed on the peripheries of the metropolitan region hardly take care of the region beyond the limits of the metropolitan region. A metropolitan region may comprise area of more than one district on several occasions. Even if the metropolitan region does not comprise area from the surrounding districts, the centrepetal forces of the metropolitan area are so strong that any development within the metropolitan area should be given due consideration in the surrounding district plans because it may have direct or indirect impact. Under such circumstances the development within the metropolitan region should not ignore the affects on the surrounding districts.

At present the surrounding districts which have part of their area under the metropolitan region hardly care to integrate their district plans with the plan of the metropolitan region. Thus, the new towns or expanded towns or industrial estates which are supposed to serve as counter-magnets are left only to solve the metropolitan congestion and expansion. The towns on the peripheries of the metropolitan region will not only serve as counter-magnets to the metropolitan growth but influence much larger area beyond the metropolitan region. These aspects are not taken into consideration mainly due to the isolation of metropolitan planning in the overall network of national and State planning. Thus, there is a lack of continuity between urban and rural planning. If the district plans are comprehensive and strongly integrate the metropolitan planning, then many of the above-mentioned defects could be overcome. This is not to deny the importance of urban planning but to avoid isolated planning of urban areas.

The rapid growth of the world's urban population is unlikely to generate many new cities. Most of the growth will occur through the growth of existing centres. This is because urban centres already exist at most choice locations and the expansion of these centres is a less costly alternative than the creation of new centres.[1]

In view of the rapid growth of the metropolitan cities whatever may be the strategy for the dispersal of major investments by the government, there is less hope of curbing their growth rate in the near future. This has been proved in the case of metropolitan cities like Calcutta, Bombay, Madras and Bangalore. The major industrial investments create scale economics which no private entrepreneur would like to lose, and the result is the agglomeration of industries around the urban centre. So the positive approach is to plan their organisation and regulate the growth.

Stressing the same and bringing the positive outlook, Turner writers: "In the sprawling cities of the Third World, there is a great need for the creation of new towns within the urban fabric. There is a need in such cities for community building in the best sense and not just the creation of new and inaccessible housing projects. The proposed urban structure combines the scale and convenience of medium-sized cities with access to the range of opportunities and special resources that can only be found in a metropolis."[2]

These newly planned communities have got a vital role to play in the metropolitan outgrowth. There are several instances when the work centres came up without housing and houses built without work centres. This is mainly due to the lack of understanding of the work-home relationship and improper integration among the various urban development bodies. The questions like whether a new town or expanded town on the peripheries of the metropolitan region should be a satellite town or ring town or dormitory town are repeatedly asked, forgetting the essential purpose in the construction of new town as formulated in the development plan. The planners and critics should self-examine the application of these concepts and instead of pressing the satisfactory answer for the concept they should concentrate on solving the problems. Planners cannot relax on theoretical concepts when the growth of metropolitan cities is fast and the cure is a necessity. These cities can no longer lose time and options for prolonged intellectual debates and discussions.

Doxiadis has rightly pointed out that the cities are no longer static and, with the flowing energy, they are becoming more dynamic and there is no ideal size for the growth of the city. The pace of growth of these cities could be reduced but not the growth rate in total. So, for a growing city the organisation of growing activities is essential. Models and experiences from the West can be borrowed but their interpretation should be made indigenous and the wholesale transplantation should be given up.

There is a mystique about the term 'new town' which is perhaps unfortunate. Use of the term conjures up images of large development corporations and high standards of environment and amenity.[3] The development of newly planned communities involves several organisations and their integration. They are built over a length of time, and the prevailing socio-economic evils cannot be mitigated by new area development because the quality of population and the activities performed remain almost the same. Whatever mistakes are committed earlier in the metropolitan cities could be avoided because of the opportunity to organise on a comparatively small scale. It should be seen that they are properly integrated into the metropolitan city and effectively linked to the metropolitan services.

Statement of the Problem

The trend of rapid economic development and increasing population of Hyderabad and its horizontal expansion call for an early formulation of policy regarding the development of the region. In view of this there is a proposal to develop four ring towns, viz., Ramachandrapuram, Shamshabad, Ghatkesar and Nedchal, around Hyderabad city by the local development authority to act as semi-counter magnets of the city's economic development.

The present study tries to examine the justification of the proposal contents made in the 'Development Plan of Hyderabad' with reference to Ramachandrapuram as ring town. It tries to see whether it can satisfy the proposal, and to achieve that, the kind of planning approach and development policies needed in the Ramachandrapuram-Patancheruvu zone.

Objectives of the Study

The following objectives are formulated to satisfy the study goal :

(a) To study the urban growth implications and selected planning concepts adopted for town planning.
(b) To study the important problems of metropolitan growth and new town attempts made around the metropolitan cities with special reference to India.
(c) To study the 'Hyderabad Development Area' briefly with regard to the zones and delineation, and the ring town strategy envisaged in the 'Development Plan of Hyderabad'.
(d) To study the growth of Ramachandrapuram-Patancheruvu zone.
(e) To find the regional influence of Ramachandrapuram after the establishment of BHEL factory with reference to the occupation structure.
(f) Finding the major demographic changes in Ramachandrapuram zone between the decade 1961-71.
(g) To find out the functional classification and centrality of each village in Ramachandrapuram zone.
(h) To adopt a planning approach and suggest indicative development policies for Ramachandrapuram-Patancheruvu area.

Methodology

The study is basically dependent on the secondary data available due to the limited time and manpower. The essential data was collected from the following sources :

— Initial ring town proposal and relevant maps on Ramachandrapuram-Patancheruvu zone and other details were collected from Hyderabad Urban Development Authority.
— The proposed industrial development at Patancheruvu was collected from Andhra Pradesh Industrial Infrastructure Corporation and the Industrial Development Officer, Industrial Estate, Patancheruvu.
— The established industries and total workers employed in and around Ramachandrapuram and Patancheruvu was obtained from the Director of Industries, Andhra Pradesh, Hyderabad.
— Census reports of 1961 and 1971 from the Census of India, Andhra Pradesh, Hyderabad, was used for the analysis of Ramachandrapuram region and zone.
— Personal visits to the site, *Panchayat*, personal talks with the local people and authorities helped a lot in the study.
— In addition to all this, the relevant literature study on the subject helped in understanding the problem and building up the work.

The study was made in two parts. In the first part, the theoretical base was built on the literature study and the relevant secondary data available on the growth of Ramachandrapuram-Patancheruvu.

In the case study part the influence region of Ramachandrapuram was found on the basis of census reports showing the nearest town to a village. Thus, the villages showing Ramachandrapuram township as the nearest town were included in the region and the impact was found. The Spatial Lorenz Curve was used to find out the changes in the spatial distribution of economic activities. The demographic changes were found on the basis of the census reports for the years 1961 and 1971 of both Medak and Hyderabad districts because Ramachandrapuram zone includes the village of both the districts.

The functional classification and centrality of each village was found on the basis of the mean and standard deviation to know the functional specialisation and functional centrality in the years 1961 and 1971

The planning approach was based on the evaluations discussed and the indicative development policies were suggested for the area based on the analysis.

NOTES

1. Turner Alan (1980). *The Cities of the Poor*, Croom Helm, London.
2. *Ibid.*
3. *Ibid.*

2

NEW TOWN ATTEMPTS IN METROPOLITAN PLANNING

THE URBAN growth is alarming in India. Though the urbanisation, the percentage of urban population to total population in demographic terms, is not very high but the absolute number of urban population is very high.

One of the significant features of the 1981 Census is the slight decline in the growth rate of population from 24.80 per cent to 24.75 per cent in 1981. The metropolitan cities accounted for five per cent of the total population of the country in the 1971 Census, but now they account for 6.08 per cent of the total population. The cities which have crossed the million mark after the 1971 Census are Pune, Nagpur, Lucknow and Jaipur raising the number of metropolitan cities from eight to 12 in 1981.[1]

Urban Growth and Problems of the Metropolitan Cities

The main reason for the increase in urban population is migration, and it is not from rural areas alone but from smaller towns to larger towns. Villages are not getting transformed into urban centres, but existing urban centres are attracting more population. This phenomenom is well illustrated in the Table 2.1.

In 1971 more than 52 per cent of urban population lived in Class I cities. The Class II, III and IV had 42 per cent of the urban population. Thus 94 per cent of the population live in cities having more than 10,000 persons. The balance is found in Class V and VI towns.

Stressing the need of urbanisation it was emphasized that the process of urbanisation is not only desirable but essential for generating economic growth and social change in India.[2]

TABLE 2.1 : Class of Towns in India

Size	Category	Population Percentage		No. of Towns	
		1961	1971	1961	1971
I	100,000 +	48.37	52.42	107	142
II	50,000 - 99,999	11.89	14.15	139	198
III	20,000 - 49,999	18.53	17.36	518	617
IV	10,000 - 19,999	13.03	12.04	820	931
V	5,000 - 9,999	7.23	5.24	848	756
VI	Less than 5,000	0.95	0.80	268	277

(*Source :* Bose Ashish, '*India's Urbanisation 1901-2001*').

If urbanisation is a process which is essential then can we do something about the heavy migration to the cities and stop the migrants to reduce the urban problems? No, because the rural-urban migration is a planned move of a group that represents one of the most valuable human resources of an otherwise poor country.[3] So the inevitable urbanisation process, heavy urban immigration and rapid urban growth led to several problems in the metropolitan cities. The problems may be briefly summed up as below :

Traffic and Transportation

The increasing vehicle ownership, the roads which were not meant for fast moving traffic, the encroachments on the narrow streets, the agglomeration of commercial activities in streets and lanes where the traffic cannot ply, the increasing traffic bottlenecks and accidents at the intersections, increasing number of commuters from long distances and fast expanding city areas pose several transportation problems. These problems are not purely technological but they are closely inter-linked with several other problems.

Overcrowding

It is very difficult to sum up the difficulties of overcrowding. Louis Wirth has rightly put it that a city is a large, dense and heterogeneous collection of people. The density of population creates several problems. The densities are high in the core and in the poor people living areas. The increasing densities without any amenities and facilities and the vast low densities in the outlaying area increase the cost of infrastructure, really pose a challenge to the growing metropolitan cities. Overcrowding of activities at a particular place, like Colaba in Bombay, create several problems with the growth of the city. Certain de-centralisation and re-distribution of function are always necessary to avoid such problems.

Slums and Shortage of Housing

The unpreparedness of the urban areas to receive the new migrants created several problems in the spheres of employment and housing. The acceptance and legalisation of informal sector and hutments are still a big question. Housing and environment are not the major problems for the poor people alone, it is equally true in the case of other sections of the population also. Several housing projects have been undertaken so far, but little thinking has been given to the question of organisation. Houses are just built and sold like commodity, but the increasing need for rented houses and high rental values are ignored in tackling the housing problem. A rigorous housing policy should be devised at the lowest level with a broad directive from the top.

Pollution

Pollution of air and water is increasing with the increasing industrial and commercial activities. The smoke, the dust, the solid waste, the polluted food and water have almost become part of urban dwellers life. Some kind of pollution appears inevitable in our brick and concrete cities, but there is a need to check this increasing pollution which may affect the health standards of the urban dwellers very badly. the sewage treatment plants, efficient solid waste disposal, re-designing of vehicles which leave lot of smoke on the walking pedestrains, cutting the increasing noise and preventive measures on industrial pollutants are the immediate steps necessary to reduce the increasing pollution.

Public Participation

Lack of public participation and reluctant attitude of the citizens to participate in the city development are the main drawbacks. Our Municipalities and Municipal Corporations are just bodies for the sake of name with less power and action. The active participation of Municipal Corporation in the city affairs and development programmes is necessary. The civic exhibitions and civic bodies with elected leaders are very important in the large metropolitan cities. Illiteracy need not be an obstacle to convey the message in these days of highly developed mass communication systems in the cities. The films, radio, TV and posters can take a long way to create a consciousnes_ about the city among the citizens. It is not only their awareness but also their participation in the shape of their elected leaders which is very important for active urban development. One cannot keep the people as spectators any longer because citizens make the city and if they lack co-operative spirit it will decay.

Planning Strategies for Metropolitan Cities

There is general agreement among all the planners that something should be done to bring about the necessary changes in the metropolitan cities and suggest a pattern of growth for large urban agglomerations by which the problems mentioned above could be minimised.

On the one hand are the views of the economists, who point out that the growth of metropolitan areas has resulted from the need of industrial specialisation and agglomeration economies, and hence the continued growth of metropolis is necessary if economic progress is to be maintained. On the other hand are the views of the physical planners who argue that in the interest of quality of life in urban areas, the growth of metropolis should be restricted. Between these two extreme points of view are the views of those who suggest that the growth of metropolitan areas should be maintained but the growth should be guided on 'desirable' lines.[4]

Several strategies have been evolved and implemented keeping in view the different opinions expressed so far. Some of them have suggested new towns or expanded town as satellite or ring towns within the metropolitan region. It had been assumed that these new towns could reduce the impact of rapid growth on the metropolis by absorbing a substantial proportion of expected increase in urban population. In some other areas strategies have been suggested with emphasis on growth nodes beyond the metropolitan region. Quite separate from these strategies, some suggested a continued expansion of the existing metropolitan areas and emphasis has been on finding a desirable form of metropolitan growth.

Focusing the attention on the first strategy of developing new towns and expanded towns around the metropolis, the aim was mainly to fulfil two major roles :

(a) To take the spill over population of the metropolitan areas, and
(b) To develop their economic base in terms of industries and offices so as to become self-contained in certain aspects and reduce the long commuting distances.

The criticism is that the attempts of new town's development succeeded in the first and failed in the second role. In view of several such criticisms the new town development is always open to question.

Early New Town Attempts Around the Metropolitan Cities

As the existing factories and businesses in the big and more established cities expanded and hired more workers, the cities grew. The housing shortage became worse. Community facilities, such as, water, schools and roads, became overloaded. When it appeared that the limits of space, efficiency and human endurance were being reached, some means had to be found to distribute industry and population over a wider area. Interest increased in an idea which was adopted in England during the 19th century – the Development of New Towns.[5]

Thus the conception of new town was a rescue measure because people want to get away from the increasing problems of the existing cities. This idea was very well conceived by Ebenezer Howard, leading later to the 'Garden City Movement'.

To define the garden city, "A garden city is a town designed for healthy living and industry, of a size which makes possible a full measure of social life, but not larger: surrounded by a rural belt: the whole of the land being in public ownership or held in trust for the community."[6]

Ebenezer Howard carried forward his ideas in Letchworth and Welwyn garden cities around London to reduce the pressure of population in London and also to test and prove that his garden cities would be successful if properly implemented. Though the success of these two garden cities is a controversial issue, it led to the passing of New Towns Act in 1946 by British Government (Map 2.1).

MAP 2.1 : Proposals of the Greater London

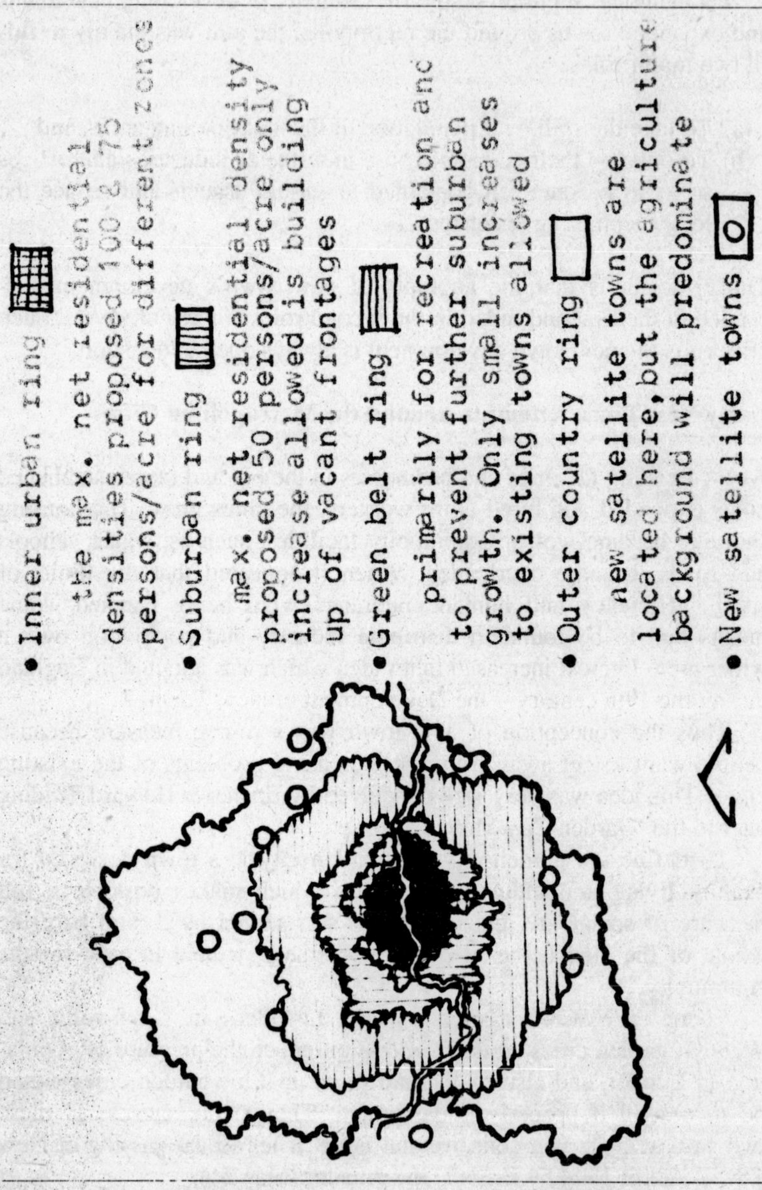

Source: Town & Country Planning & Housing - - Modak & Ambdekar

The first major application of new town construction was proposed by Patrick Abercrombie who suggested the development of series of new towns to be established within a radius of 25 to 30 miles from London. These new towns were intended to absorb the industry and the population from the overcrowded parts of the metropolis. This idea was accepted by the Great Britain Government and a committee, known as 'New Towns Committee', was appointed on whose recommendations the New Towns Act was passed.

According to this Act the then Town and Country Planning Ministry got the power to designate any area of land as a site for new town and appoint a development corporation charged with the development and lay-out of the new town.

The success of the new town movement in England has been severely criticised and many a time it ended up as a mere extension suburb of the existing city. In view of several such controversial issues on new town building, the application of garden city concept raised many doubts.

Defending the garden city concept and condemning the faulty application of the idea, Mumford says : "The garden city do not imply either isolation or parochial self-containment, in the fashion of a sleepy country town in a remote inaccessable area. He felt that it was enough if there was sufficient concentration of economic opportunities and social interests to keep most of the inhabitants fully occupied, for most of the time, in an environment that possessed many positive urban values that London itself could no longer give even to the wealthy."[7]

One of the important contributions derived from the garden city is the neighbourhood concept evolved by Clarence Stein and Henry Wright and successfully applied in new town building everywhere with different expressions. The population ranges of the unit differ from country to country. In India it could be taken as four or five thousand persons.

In a properly planned lay-out of a neighborhood unit, a school-going child does not have to walk for more than five to ten minutes to reach the primary school in complete safety. The housewife too does not have to cover long distances to purchase daily necessities of life.[8] An important feature is that all roads carrying town traffic run around its periphery and none across it so that the inhabitants are completely free from traffic hazards.

The neighbourhood unit is made the smallest unit for new town planning to stimulate community life. This forms a part of next larger unit called as sector. Several such sectors form a town. The facilities at each level are provided depending upon the threshold population and accessibility. The segregation of pedestrian and vehicular traffic is another important aspect seriously considered in new town planning.

The new town planning in India is followed in line with the British new town planning. There are over hundred new towns built in India for several purposes. They can be broadly classified into the following categories :

(a) Capital towns,
(b) Refugee towns,
(c) Industrial towns,
(d) Port towns,
(e) Satellite towns.

All these towns have been constructed with a single purpose and do not try to integrate the surrounding region. The advantages of deliberate urbanisation and economic development on a larger scale have been given less thought in the planning of these towns. The criticism on new town development around the metropolitan city is totally different. The problems of fast metropolitan growth and the need to develop the new areas around the metropolitan city should be viewed in a different perspective.

Since the new towns in India are planned in line with new towns in Britain and USA, because of similar governmental structure and large investments in building the new towns, the evaluations done on Britain and USA new towns are very useful even in India.

Evaluation of New Towns in Britain and USA

The new towns in Britain and USA are quite different because of the nature of the Government and the values of the society. British society is more hierarchical and class conscious than American society. In America the equality of the people and importance to personal attributes for success are dominant. A person is judged mainly on the basis of his own qualities rather than ancestorial inheritance.

The war time damage in Great Britain compelled the government to take active steps to radically alter the pattern of growth and the anxiousness was for large-scale change. In America, the private initiative is more in the absence of well-defined urban policy. In Britain it was the development corporations which took pains to create and construct the new towns whereas in America the private developers assumed the major responsibility for building planned communities.

The British new town had mixed success in the spheres of economic development and administration. The town residents appeared to have showed general satisfaction on the new physical environment whereas there are indications of conflicts between members of the development corporations and elected local government officials, and also between the new town residents and the old communities.

Public involvement in new town building is very limited in America, so the private developers are mainly interested in their profits to serve their own purposes. The American new towns are meant for middle-income and upper-income groups only. They are not having enough economic base to support themselves independently. So they are just rich environments meant to suit the needs of certain section of the people without meeting any regional needs and built in disregard with the nearby urban areas.

Comparing the British and American programmes to-date, the former appears to have achieved greater success than the latter in building new towns. Not only has it produced more towns, housing, factory and retail units, but – relative to the US programmes – it has more successfully fulfilled the criteria of social balance and autonomy, thus contributing to regional development and urban de-centralisation.[9]

Another important aspect of British new towns is that they have done little to the de-centralisation of employment and population from the capital city, and most of them have taken of suburban additions to the existing towns.

Three important trends of British new town policy at present are:[10]

a. The emphasis on private-public partnership in new town building.
b. The emphasis on town expansion as opposed to new town development.
c. The emphasis on eliminating regional imbalances as opposed to an urban problem orientation in the implementation of the programme.

The weakness of American new towns is the absence of national urban policy and the predominance of profit mindedness among the private builders. Neither American nor English new towns contributed for urban de-congestion, alteration of urban growth and urban renewal. The emphasis of British new towns on their development is as growth centres in the rural areas and as counter-magnets to large metropolitan centres.

The poor public service and squatting are the main problems of any new town, which look at the town as a neat environment problem. Criticising the planners' approach to Brasilia, the capital city of Brazil, an anthropologist points out :

> The rise and persistance of the squatter settlements in Brasilia are a manifestation of the structural characteristics of Brazilian society, so also we suggest that squatting is not amenable to eradication by any administrative or financial measures within the reach of those responsible for the government of the new capital, for so long as the basic structure of the society persuits."[11]

Bringing the importance of service workers another author raises a question :

> "The service workers are owners of small stores, repair shops and so on. They do not make much money, but they are independent and they get by. They line, the side streets and secondary avenues of every city. Our new plans make no provision for these people. Where are they to go, what are they to go?"[12]

Housing is an important question. It is not always necessary that everybody should live in *pucca* cement concrete structure. The high-rise technology and sophisticated technology are not the answers for housing the population in under-developed countries. Mother Earth in the shape of mud is a solution to house the millions in the under-developed countries. Housing is not a problem of floor, wall and roof alone, it has something to do with the stratified society and the distributive justice and the enforced government policies. Nobody in Shanghai, China, sleeps on the roads and pavements of the crowded city and houses are no better than tin, plywood, card-board sheds and no one is without a roof of some kind.[13] This clearly reveals the role of societal values and political ideologies in providing the housing facilities. There is every need in India to understand and assimilate the existence of slums and squatments, hawkers and vendors, and other informal sector in organising the city development programmes. Uprooting or displacing shows only hollowness in conceiving the urban society.

Evaluation of Indian New Towns

The genuine criticism raised against the new town development in India is that there are over hundred new townships constructed in India and majority of them are just company townships that were appendages to an industry rather than towns serving a region. One acre plots for single family dwellings were common not to talk about the low densities. In many new towns a sizeable segment of the industrial labour has to commute long distances. Innovation was limited to devising housing types, and very little thought has been given to the evolutionary aspects of housing. The new towns offered scope for the development of ancillary and small industries, besides other economic activities, which are not considered in depth. The socio-economic characteristics and potentials of the surrounding region are not explored. Industrial management has been quite reluctant to accept Municipal institutions with people's elected representatives in the townships for the fear of tax whereas they are saddled with the job of running their estates and colonies. It is useful to examine the new town development around the major metropolitan cities like Bombay, Calcutta and Madras at the juncture.

The Proposal to Develop New Bombay Township Near Bombay

The increasing problems of Bombay, like, over-congestion, pollution, heavy commutation, traffic and transportation pressure, inadequate civic amenities and growing slums, led to the constitution of the Bombay Metropolitan Regional Planning Board by the State, in 1967, to study and plan the future of Bombay in the regional context (Map 2.2).

The plan proposals include the layout of new township in the trans-Thana Creek area, a twin-city or the Metro Centre, development of industrial growth poles, such as, Kalyan, Kolshet-Balkhun, Khopoli, Mira-Bhyandar and Apte-Turade complexes, regulation of industrial locations, augmentation and re-alignment of the existing rail and road networks internally and in relation to adjoining areas, and provision of a new port.[14]

The new urban complex (or New Bombay) will be flanked on one side by the existing and growing industrial complex of Kalwa-Belapur, and on the other by a proposed residential area. The existing Thana-Belapur road and proposed one along the western flanks of the Creek will form a circuit of expressways within which the entire residential and commercial areas will be accommodated. The Bombay-Pune highway through the new bridge across the Thana Creek runs across the heart of this township west to east. The residential area is split into a number of planning districts and sectors. Each sector would possess the necessary social infrastructure and community facilities, and a group of three to four sectors would have a common district centre.

MAP 2.2 : Proposed Site of New Bombay in Bombay Metropolitan Region

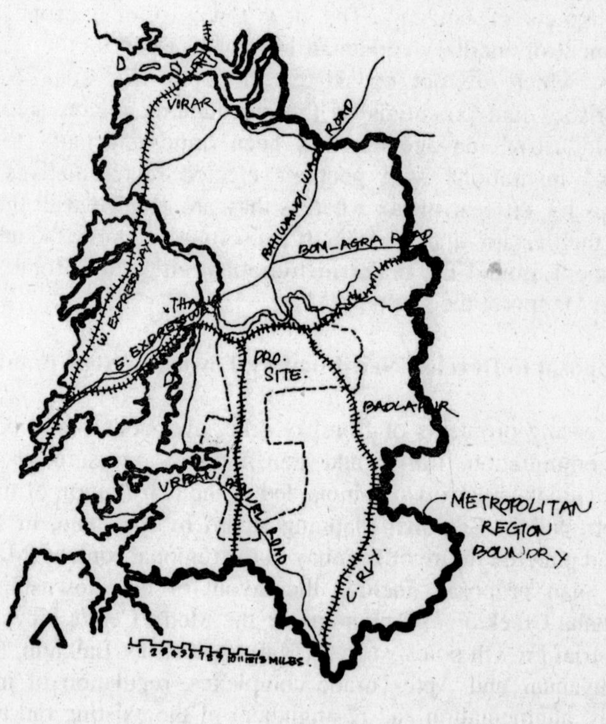

Source: Town & Country Planning & Housing — Modak & Ambdekar

The township runs north to south over a length of 20 km. It is proposed to develop three commercial zones; one in north, another in the middle and third in the south. Major playgrounds and parks are proposed in the intervening green belt so as to provide an open area of 1.5 hectares for every 1,000 people. The area of the whole stretch from Kalwa to Uran is about 5,000 hectares, and sectoral population densities of about 125 persons per hectare are envisaged for the complex as whole.

The new city will be supported by a new port at Nhava-Sheva. It will have direct access to the Bombay-Konkan highway as well as to the railway. For all practical purposes the new city will be independent of Bombay, yet part of the urban complex of the Bombay region. It is proposed to shift the administrative functions of Bombay to the new Metro Centre. The occupational structure and social composition of the new centre are yet to be assessed, but it is expected that the new city will carry the same cosmopolitan ingredients as the present city of Bombay.

Beyond the present urban complex, the regional plan will attempt to check haphazard development of housing outside the existing towns, such as dormitory centres along routeways. To relieve the port congestion, the future development is centred around Nhava-Sheva. This port will serve the dynamic needs of the emerging industrial complexes in the mainland and will divert some port traffic of the present docks to the new harbour.

New Township Proposals around Calcutta

Calcutta is the leading metropolitan city in India. There has been an endeavour by the planners to find new areas to be developed as satellite cities. In search of such areas and to take away some load from Calcutta, the Calcutta Metropolitan Development Authority developed a concept of poly-nodal growth centres. It was envisaged that such growth centres should come up on both sides of the river with proper communication linkages. They are :

(a) West Howrah Area Development Project
(b) East Calcutta township and Area Development Project.

West Howrah area Development Project

This project generates new areas of activity at the periphery of the congested core of CMD.

About 2,000 acres of land, bounded by Benares Road on the north, existing railway embankment and the Howrah drainage line on the east, proposed Kona expressway on the south and the national highways on the west, has a tremendous potential for urban development.

In the present programme of Phase I activity two projects within this total area have been taken up :

(a) West Howrah Area Development Project Phase I covering 455.5 acres.
(b) Kona truck terminal-cum-wholesale trading centre covering 218 acres.

In addition to the above two areas, about 135 acres of land on the western side of the national highway No. 6 will be used as borrowpit for filling up of the land for West Howrah Area Development Project (Phase I) and also for Kona Truck Terminal Project.

Objectives of the Scheme[15]

(i) To provide new area to absorb future metropolitan growth by creating integrated township with employment facilities.
(ii) To provide industrial sites and services to different categories of people.
(iii) To provide sites and services for residential accommodation to different groups.
(iv) To provide new community facilities promoting improved living conditions for people of all economic groups.
(v) To provide a basic frame of facilities to promote new centres in future in the adjoining areas to serve the agricultural hinterland.
(vi) To provide a basic frame of facilities to support the creation of wholesale trading centre-cum-truck terminal in the adjoining areas to syphon off the pressure from the congested CBD.

Beneficiaries : The West Howrah Area Development Project in its first phase will be able to hold a population of about 50,000. The project will provide about 75,000 ownership plots and about 1,000 rental units. In addition there would be a large area (144 acres) for developing industrial estate and similar facilities for promoting economic activity.

East Calcutta Township and area Development Project

The area is hardly 15 km from the central business district of Calcutta and it is linked to the core by the eastern metropolitan bypass. Care has been taken to see that the township does not grow in isolation but offers a well-knit pattern. Thus, apart from residential buildings and plots for various categories of people, there is provision for colonies, specially meant for the working class, like, washermen, milkmen and fishermen. There is also provision for industrial estates and markets.

Though East Calcutta will emerge as a predominantly residential township, care has been taken to ensure that the major beneficiaries are from the low-income category of the people.

MAP 2.3 : Sketch Showing New Town Proposal around Madras

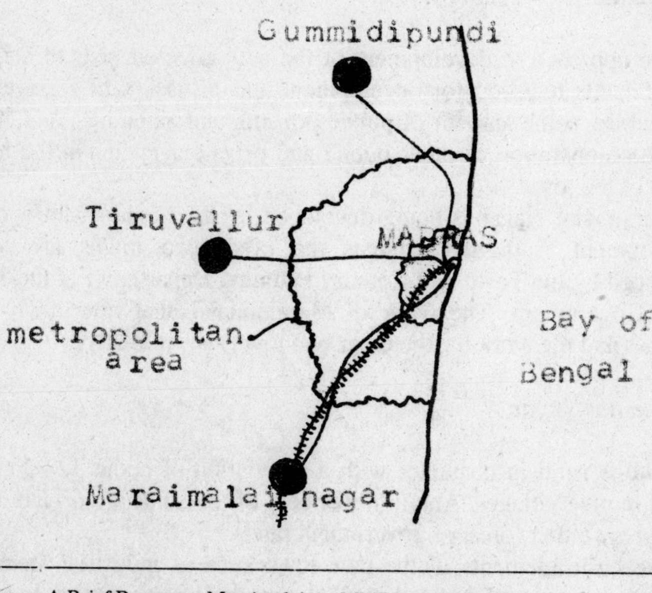

Source: A Brief Report on Maraimalai — MMDA, Madras

The township will accommodate about 40,000 people and covers an area of about 475 acres in the first phase out of the available 667 acres. Necessary provisions for primary, secondary schools, health clinics, markets, police station, fire station, post office, community centres and industrial estates are being made. The villages for washermen, fishermen, and milkmen will be on the east of the eastern metropolitan bypass. There is provision for keeping 5,000 cattle and use of cowdung for bio-gas generation. Suitable credit facilities will be extended for repayment for the low-income and economically weaker sections.

New Town Proposals around Madras

The Master Plan for Madras has spelt out a strategy for development of three new towns to serve as counter-magnets to check migration into the Madras Metropolitan Area (Map 2.3). Gummadipundi in the north, Tinwallur in the east and Maraimalai Nagar in the south are the three proposed new towns.[16]

The new town of Maraimalai Nagar is located 43 km from Madras. It is being developed on virgin land and is designed to have ultimately a population of 100,000 by 1991.

The approach to development of the new town consists of acquisition of lands required for development and provision of required infrastructure, some amount of public housing and amenities, and enlisting the co-operation of other public and private agencies in the building up of the town.

Maraimalai Nagar is being developed by the Madras Metropolitan Development Authority whereas the other two towns are to be developed by the Town and Country Planning Department of the Tamil Nadu Government. The work of Maraimalai Nagar new town is in progress and the work for the other two towns is yet to start.

Maraimalai Nagar

The site is rural in character with a population of about 12,000 comprised in nine villages. About 50 per cent of the lands are private while the rest are either forest or government lands.

The basic elements of the new town such as industrial areas, the residential neighourhoods, the town centre, the recreation and park areas and the transport system will be well integrated and the town designed in such a way that future expansion becomes easy and will merge harmoniously with the previous development.

The new town will have diversified economic base providing employment in industries, trade and commerce, services with importance to industrial employment.

The hierarchy of town units comprises groups of dwellings with required social facilities located as close to the dwellings as possible at the first level, to be repeated to form a residential neighbourhood. At the second level, a number of residential neighbourhoods are grouped around a town centre with varied facilities like offices, shopping centres, cinemas, etc., which are frequently needed by the people. In order to avoid congestion, the focal points of the town, such as, the town centre, the industrial area and the institutional area, are distributed with living areas provided in-between.

NOTES

1. Padmanabha, P. (1981). 'A Note on the Provisional Results of 1981 Census of India', *Yojana*, 16-30 May.
2. Bose Ashish (1978). *India's Urbanisation 1901-2001*, Tata McGraw-Hill Publishing Co. Ltd., New Delhi.
3. Koenighsberger Otto (1976). "Issue in Urban Development", Institute of Development Studies, Mysore.
4. Ansari, H. Jamal (1975-76). "A Review of Strategies for Physical planning of Metropolitan areas", *Journal of Institute of Town Pianner*, India, December and March.
5. Abrams Charles (1964). *Man's Struggle for shelter in an urbanising world*, Vakils, Peffer and Scimons Pvt. Ltd., Bombay.
6. Mac Fadyen Dugald (1970). *Sir Ebenezer Howard and the Town Planning Movement*, the MIT Press, Massachusetts.
7. Mumford Lewis (1961). *The City in History*, Seckar E. Wasburg, London.
8. Modak E. Ambedekar (1971). *Town and Country Planning and Housing*, Orient Longman Ltd., Madras.
9. Cardon Card (1977). *Planned Cities*, Sage Publications, London.
10. *Ibid.*
11. Epstein G. David (1973). *Brascilia — Plan and Reality*, Univerity of California Press, London, Los Angles.
12. Woodbury Edeman (1974). *The Future of Cities and Urban Development*, University of Chicago Press, Chicago & London, Reprint.
13. Chopra, S.N. (1981). 'China Diary — IV', *New Delhi Magazine*, March 16-29.
14. Arunachalam, A.B. (1978). 'Bombay: an exploding metropolis' from edited Misra, R.P. *Million Cities of India*, Vikas Publishing House Pvt. Ltd., Bombay.
15. Obtained from a Pamphlet of the Calcutta Metropolitan Development Authority, Calcutta.
16. Details obtained from a Pamphlet 'Maraimalai Nagar, New Town' by Madras Metropolitan Development Authority, Madras.

3

INTRODUCTION TO HYDERABAD DEVELOPMENT AREA

HYDERABAD IS a leading metropolitan city of Andhra Pradesh and the primate city of Telangana region.

In most countries there is one city, almost invariably the capital, which is much bigger and presents a greater range of activities than any other city. Mark Jefferson calls such cities as primate and his law that a country's leading city is always proportionately large and exceptionally expressive of national capacity and feeling is more applicable to agricultural developing countries.[1]

Though Hyderabad is not the only leading city in the country, but it is the only leading metropolitan city of the State. The major asset of Hyderabad city is that it is the capital of Andhra Pradesh and possesses highly specialised educational, commercial, medical and administrative services. Besides the Osmania, Central, Agricultural and Technological Universitities, it has advanced research and training centres of national and international importance in Chemistry, Geo-Physics, Nutrition, Electronics, Public Enterprise, American Studies, Rural Development, Small industries, Forensic Medicine, Banking and Personnel Management and Survey and Photogrammetry. It has two branches of all the leading banks in the country. It is also the headquarters of South-Central Railway zone. The major industries located in Hyderabad are Hindustan Aeronautics Limited, Bharat Heavy Electricals Limited, Hindustan Machine Tools, Praga Tools and Electronics Corporation of India Limited. Besides this, it has got major institutions like Regional Research Laboratories, Indian Drugs and Pharmaceuticals Limited, International Crops Research Institute for Semi-Arid Tropics, etc.

Developing Urban System in Andhra Pradesh

Before going into the regional influence of Hyderabad metropolis, a brief understanding of the developing urban system in Andhra Pradesh would be useful.

There are four important urban regions developing in Andhra Pradesh :

1. Hyderabad urban region covering the Telangana area.
2. Vijayawada-Guntur urban region covering the delta areas of the coastal Andhra.
3. Vishakhapatnam urban region covering the districts Srikakulam, Vizianagram and Vishakhapatnam.
4. Kurnool-Nellore urban region which covers the entire Rayalaseema region.

The largest area of influence goes to the Hyderabad urban region followed by Kurnool-Nellore, Vijayawada-Guntur, and Vishakhapatnam urban regions. The peculiarities in the development of these four urban regions are pin-pointed below :

(a) Vishakhapatnam is the smallest region. The high industrialisation in Vishakhapatnam is likely to develop external economic links in the future. However, the tribal society of the region's vast forest area constitutes the main problem.

(b) Kurnool-Nellore has got the highest number of small towns, and consequently less share of State's urban population. In absence of a distinct production specialisation centre to link it with other regions, it may be further cut-off from the former as urbanisation proceeds. The two main problems are absence of hierarchy of urban centres and lack of good transportation network.

(c) Vijayawada-Guntur is the most prosperous agricultural region in the country. Along with this it developed good agro-based industries. The percentage share of urban population in total population in the region is the highest for any region in the State.

(d) Hyderabad urban region has got the most unevenly developed economic space in the State. The polarisation of development towards the metropolis and the integration between the region and the metropolis are the major problems of the urban region.

Delineated Hyderabad Metropolitan Region

The influence of metropolitan Hyderabad over Telangana is more directly exercised by its distributive activities such as circulation of newspapers, wholesale selling in tea, textiles, general merchandise, timber, drugs and pharmaceuticals and centralised services like medical and educational.

What is meant by the terms "Metropolitan" and "Region"? Both terms imply that there is a set of areal or spatial units which transcends the limits of an individual city or urban place and which have sufficient functional and physical integrity to justify the consideration in the planning process.[2]

Thus, within the larger influence area an area surrounding the metropolis could be de-limited wherein there is a close interaction between the city and other settlements economically, socially and spatially. In order to define precisely the boundary of the Hyderabad metropolitan region, a study was made in the Hyderabad Metropolitan Research Project with certain key urban functions.

The indicators which were taken for the delineation are as follows :

1. Circulation of daily newspapers.
2. University education : distribution pattern of resident scholars.
3. Range and frequency of bus services.
4. Supply zone of vegetables.
5. Milk supply zone.
6. Supply of fruits.
7. Grape cultivation zone.

The delineated metropolitan region of Hyderabad is as shown in Map 3.1. The important urban centres are Bhongir, Sangareddy, Sadasivpet, Vicarabad Shadnagar, Ibrahimpatnam and Gajwal.

Delineation of Hyderabad Development Area

The Hyderabad metropolitan region is too extensive to be treated as a planning area, though it can be used for broad economic planning. There is a core area of metropolitan impact in which a number of rural settlements contiguous to the incorporated area are slowly getting urbanised.

Almost every city has, outside its potential boundaries, residential or commercial or manufacturing areas, large or small, which are economically a part of the central community, sharing its fortunes and needing to co-operate in the policies. The larger area, containing both the city proper and the outlying activities, must, therefore, for its best effectiveness, be planned as a unit.[3] These areas are served by metropolitan based services like transport, retailing, water supply, electricity, etc. This area can be treated as the primary planning area for the metropolitan city.

MAP 3.1: Hyderabad Metropolitan Region

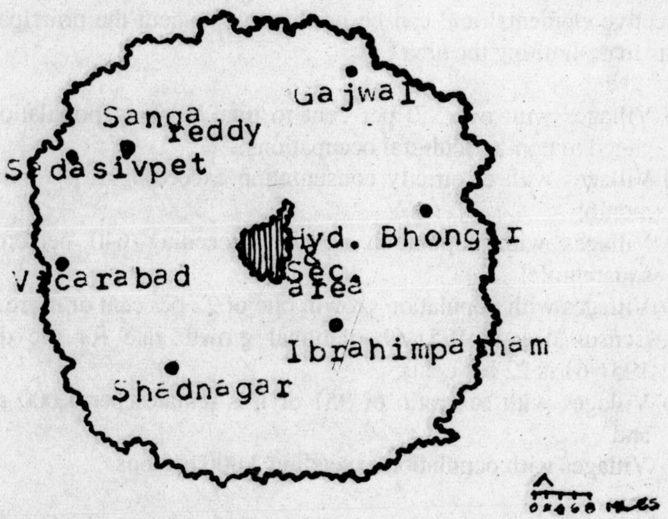

* Area : 4257.75 Sq.miles
* No. of villages: 1560
* Density: 316 per sq.miles
* Population: 26,57,929
* Employment: 11,63,624
(figs as per 1961 census)

Source: The Hyderabad Metropolitan Research Project Report — Manzoor Alam

In order to define precisely the boundary of the planning area, the impact of key urban functions, which are typical of metropolitan centres, are significant indicators of daily inter-action of the metropolis with its immediate region. These functions have been termed as the 'principal elements'.[4]

(a) Suburban transport service
(b) Commuting areas of workers to factories
(c) Retailing business
(d) Water supply
(e) Telephones
(f) Postal services

In addition to these functions, metropolitan influence on the immediate rural hinterland can also be measured by examining the distributive pattern, by villages, of certain demographic and occupational characteristics which are susceptible to urban influence and reflect the intensity of urbanisation trends. These variables have been called 'reflective elements' and can be used to supplement the principal elements in de-limiting the area.[5]

(a) Villages with over 50 per cent to total working population engaged in non-agricultural occupations;
(b) Villages with electricity consumption exceeding 1,000 units per month;
(c) Villages with population density exceeding 640 persons per square mile;
(d) Villages with population growth rate of 22 per cent or more in the Census decade 1951-61 (national growth rate for the decade 1951-61 is 22 per cent);
(e) Villages with sex ratio of 951 or less females per 1,000 males; and
(f) Villages with population exceeding 2,000 persons.

The area was de-limited on the basis of 1961 Census in the research report, but the inter-action of Hyderabad city with the rural hinterland increased by 1971 leading to the increase in the area de-limited. The area thus delineated after the establishment of Hyderabad Urban Development Authority in 1975 for planning purposes is known as the Hyderabad development area.

Details of the Hyderabad Development Area

The Hyderabad development area is divided into two parts (Map 3.2). The first part is the incorporated area of the Municipal Corporation of Hyderabad-Secunderabad and the Cantonment area. The second part is the peripheral area excluding the incorporated area in the Hyderabad development area.

As per the land-use survey conducted by the Director of Town Planning in the year 1967, the land-use for the city and its environs at that time were analysed in Table 3.1.

TABLE 3.1 : Area under each of the Land-uses in Hyderabad City and its Environs

Landuse	*Area in acres*	*Percentage to total area*
Residential	6,657.8	13.88
Commercial	363.3	0.76
Industrial	751.1	1.57
Recreational	1,906.3	3.97
Public and Semi-Public	2,510.6	5.23
Transport and Communication	3,200.6	6.67
Vacant	18,860.5	39.32
Agricultural	8,555.3	17.84
Others	5,161.4	10.76
Total	47966.9	100.00

(*Source* : Development Plan for Hyderabad, 1975).

TABLE 3.2 : Peripheral AREA zones

Sl. No.	*Name of the zone*	*No. of villages*	*Area in sq.miles (1971)*
1.	Dundigal	6	18.56
2.	Medchal	13	25.32
3.	Shambapur	26	59.17
4.	Kukatpally	30	44.33
5.	Shamirpet	13	29.08
6.	Keesara	13	34.27
7.	Moulali	6	14.14
8.	Chengicharla	20	26.29
9.	Ghatkesar	17	37.37
10.	Hayatnagar	36	37.74
11.	Nadergul	5	16.72
12.	Kothapet	18	21.16
13.	Shamshabad	21	31.28
14.	Budwel	19	31.18
15.	Himayatnagar	9	23.51
16.	Popalguda	21	26.86
17.	Kollur	11	37.02
18.	Ramachandrapuram	23	54.73
		307	568.73

(*Source:* Ratna Naidu (1979). 'Organisational Structure of HUDA' *Nagarlok,* A ril-June, 11 & No. 2).

There are three important strategies proposed by the local development authority (Map 3.2).

(a) Construction of satellite towns,
(b) Development of ring towns,
(c) Development of growth centres around Hyderabad city.

MAP 3.2: Hyderabad Development Area

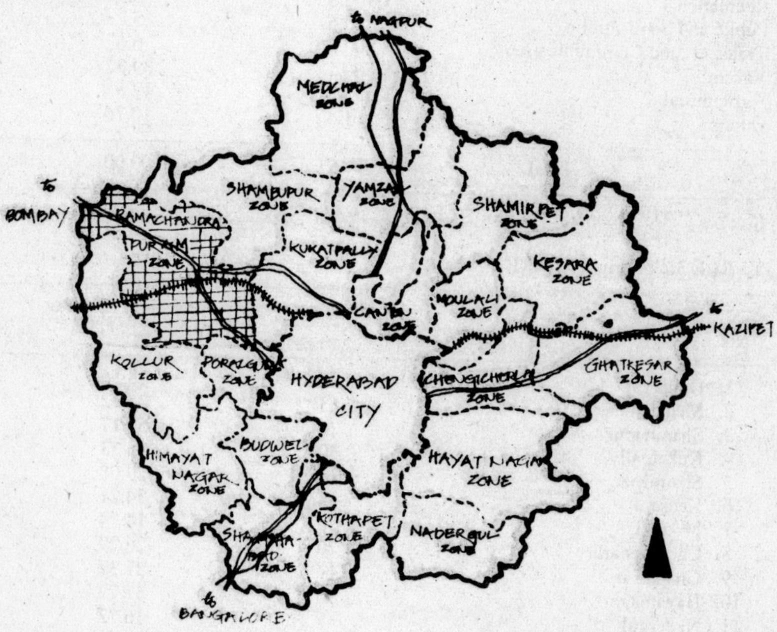

Source: Hyderabad Urban Development Authority 1981

NOTES

1. A. Jones Emrys, *Towns and Cities*, Oxford University Press

2. Claire W.M.H. (Ed.), (1973). *Handbook on Urban Planning*, Van Nostrand Keinhold Company, New York.
3. Wirth Louis, (1969). *On Cities and Social Life*, edited by Albert J. Reiss Tr., University of Chicago Press, Chicago.
4. Alam Manzoor, (1972). *Metropolitan Hyderabad & its Region*, Asia Publishing House, Madras.
5. *Ibid.*

4

THE RING TOWN STRATEGY OF HYDERABAD

THERE ARE several attempts in the metropolitan planning in India. One important strategy is the development of new town or expanded town around the metropolitan area. They have been named as new towns, satellite towns or ring towns. Whenever this kind of new area development was proposed and is being proposed, the aim has been mainly to organise the metropolitan growth. Though the purpose is never badly mentioned in the Master Plan or Development Plan, the questions like whether it satisfies the requirements of new town or satellite town or ring town are repeatedly asked.

It is high time now that instead of questioning the concepts of new town, satellite town or ring town, it is necessary to see whether the proposed new area development could really serve the purpose envisaged in the Development Plan. A metropolitan city could develop work centre or housing and other amenities wherever it is needed but the same need not be a satellite or ring or new town. These name tags often lead to misinterpretation of the purpose that is envisaged in the Development Plan. Each metropolitan city tried to solve their respective problems through new area development in a different way. When Bombay is trying to have development near the existing city, Madras is trying to plan new towns at a distance more than 40 km from the city. One strategy cannot be compared with the other because of the peculiar site and situation problems.

In the light of these observations the ring town strategy of Hyderabad is perceived with an emphasis on the purpose envisaged in the Development Plan of Hyderabad.

The Ring Town Proposal for Hyderabad City

Four ring towns are proposed by the Hyderabad Urban Development Authority around city within the limits of the Hyderabad Development area. The Development Plan says :

> "In order to understand the perspective plan of which the present Development Plan forms a part it is necessary to note the pattern proposed for setting up ring towns around the city. These towns will be located at a distance of 15 to 25 miles from the centre of the city (i.e., Nampally Station). 'Expanding towns' are to be built around the existing human settlements consisting of one or more villages. Residents of these towns will be discouraged from visiting Hyderabad in the normal course of their work and life. Special care will be taken to provide high level amenities in recreation, and to encourage people working in these towns to settle down there."[1]

This is the proposal envisaged in the Development Plan. The following areas have been proposed to be developed as ring towns :

1. Ramachandrapuram-Patancheruvu
2. Medchal
3. Ghatkesar
4. Shamshabad

Before making any comments on the ring town strategy proposed in the Hyderabad development plan, an understanding of the ring town strategy proposed earlier in the Master Plan of Delhi would be very useful.

The Ring Town Strategy of Delhi Master Plan

The Master Plan of Delhi says : "To achieve a rational growth of Delhi which has been expanding in a most haphazard way, it is necessary to plan this whole area as a composite unit and have an integrated and balanced programme of development. The six ring towns – Loni, Ghaziabad, Faridabad-Ballabhgarh, Gurgoan, Bahadurgarh and Narela – are to be developed not only to deflect some of the population that would otherwise come into Delhi and jeoparadise the planned growth of Delhi but also to help these towns to grow in a planned way. It is visualised that a compact growth of urban Delhi with six ring towns self-contained in matters of work and residential places but with strong economic, social and cultural ties with the city. This is the only way to prevent the increasing urban sprawl which is threatening to grow into one giant urban mass."[2]

The National Capital region with the location of ring towns is shown in Map 4.1. The proposals made for each ring town are briefly described below :[3]

Ghaziabad

It is located at a distance of only 16 km from Delhi. It was envisaged as an industrial town with 50,000 workers engaged in manufacturing out of a total population of about 3,57,000 in 1981. It was also proposed to diversify the economic base with an employment to 20,000 in government offices. The total area wanted to be urbanised with adequate land for residential, commercial, parks and other public and semi-public use was about 8,000 acres.

Faridabad-Ballabhgarh

It is an integrated agglomeration of three settlements of Faridabad, Ballabhgarh and Faridabad new township. It was suggested that Faridabad-Ballabhgarh should have a strong industrial base with about 43,000 workers engaged in manufacturing. It was also recommended that enough government offices be established here. The town could be served by tube-wells since it has good underground water potential.

Gurgoan

It is located at a distance of 30 km from Delhi and hardly 10 km from the Delhi border. The district town in Punjab is handicapped for want of good water source and only a modest growth was contemplated with a small industrial estate besides few government offices.

Bahadurgarh

The distance of Bahadurgarh from Delhi is about 36 km. This town has no source of good water supply. It was intended to be developed with industries requiring little water and dependent on Delhi's market.

MAP 4.1 : Ring Town Proposal of Delhi in National Capital Region

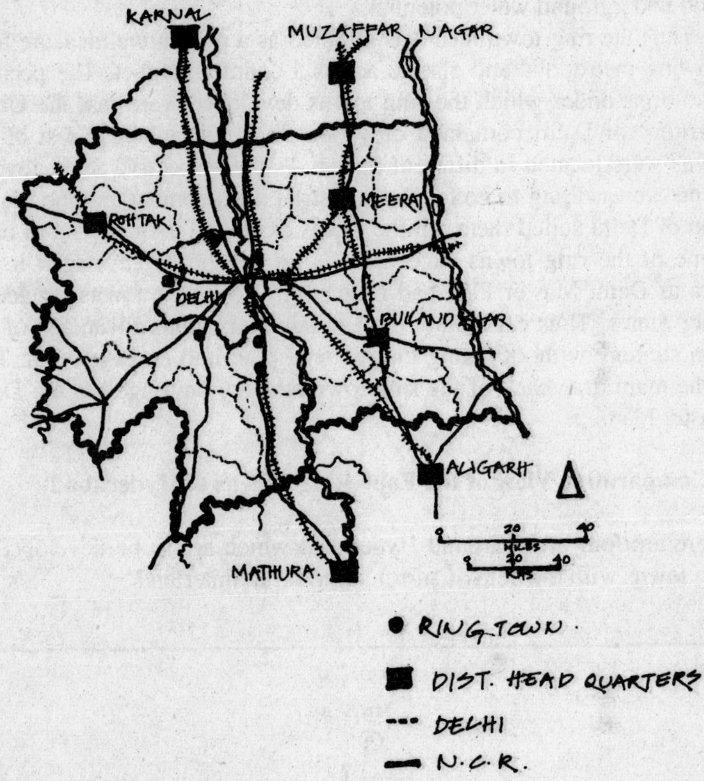

Source: Planning of Metropolitan Areas & New Towns — UN Publication, 1967

Loni

This small town was proposed to be developed with industry as an economic base. Water could be made available through tube-wells as envisaged in the Master Plan.

Narela

As recommended in the Master Plan for the Delhi metropolitan area, Narela which is within the Union Territory of Delhi and about 18 miles on the northern border of Delhi was proposed to be provided government offices and industry to make the town a self-contained unit. It has good underground water potential.

Thus the ring town idea was initiated as a preventive measure for a growing metropolis and also to act as a counter-magnet. The peculiar conditions under which the ring towns developed were that the Union Territory of Delhi contained only one ring town whereas rest of the towns were located in different States. As the respective State governments were willing to go for the industrial development and the Master Plan of Delhi suited them, all the towns expanded their industrial base. Some of the ring towns exceeded the growth limits envisaged in the plan as Delhi Master Plan had little control over the towns located in other States. Thus each State tried to take maximum advantage of the plan strategy without taking the regional plan into consideration. This is the main drawback of the ring town strategy envisaged in the Delhi Master Plan.

A Comparative View of the Four Ring Towns of Hyderabad

There are four areas around Hyderabad which are to be developed as ring towns with the help of surrounding rural hinterland.

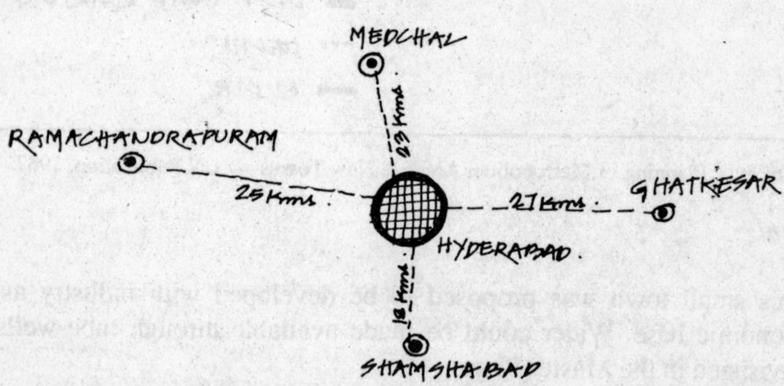

The Proposed Ring Town — a Sketch

The comparative advantage of Hyderabad over Delhi ring town strategy is that all the four towns are located within the 'Development

Area of Hyderabad'. This gives an initial advantage for integrated development of the towns by the local planning authority. But there are other difficulties like district development policies. The development area of Hyderabad comprises three districts, viz., Hyderabad, Rangareddy and Medak. Previously urban agglomeration of Hyderabad was only a part of Hyderabad district but in 1978, with the formation of Rangareddy district and Hyderabad district, Hyderabad urban agglomeration became a separate district, for administrative convenience. The rural areas and other *taluks* in the Hyderabad district are made as separate district in the name of Rangareddy. The influence of district development policies could be explained better in the case of Ramachandrapuram.

Ramachandrapuram is located in a kind of transitional zone where the metropolitan regional influence slowly reduces and the district development policies make an impact. In the existing ring town strategy of Hyderabad, the other three towns could have grown better but for the lack of certain strong district development policies. Ramachandrapuram enjoys the advantage of being located in a district which is declared by the Centre as the backward district and entitled for all kinds of political backing and development incentives. This is one of main reasons for the fast growth of the towns and the surrounding villages when compared to the other three proposed ring towns. Patancheruvu, a block headquarters in Medak district, which is located three km from Ramachandrapuram is a good case to elaborate the development policies of the district.

Patancheruvu was only a block headquarters with administrative function as the main base of the economy. Though the industrial impact of Ramachandrapuram on Patancheruvu cannot be denied but it was not as significant in 1971 as it is now. This particular village was recognised for industrial development by Andhra Pradesh Industrial Infrastructure Corporation Ltd., in 1974, and the industrial growth since then is considerable. Even though the nearness to Hyderabad city may be one criteria for industrial growth, but the same advantage of nearness did not induce similar industrial growth in the other three proposed ring towns. The initial advantages which favoured the industrial development in Patancheruvu are the agglomerated industries already existing in the surrounding villages and the attractive industrial development incentives.

It may be difficult to induce a parallel growth rate in all the four ring towns, but care should be taken to avoid extremes in the growth rates among the four towns.

Spatial Distribution of the Four Ring Towns

Ramachandrapuram and Ghatkesar are lying beside the broad-gauge line connecting Bombay and Hyderabad. Medchal and Shamshabad are lying beside the meter-gauge railway line connecting Bangalore towards the south and Manmad towards the north for the Hyderabad railway station. The general trend of growth of Hyderabad city is along the broad-gauge railway line.

Ramachandrapuram zone consists 23 villages, Shamshabad 21 villages, Ghatkesar 17 villages and Medchal 13 villages. Medchal, Ghatkesar and Shamshabad are located within the Rangareddy district whereas Ramachandrapuram is in Medak district.

The highest population zone is Ramachandrapuram followed by Ghatkesar, Shamshabad and Medchal. The density of population for each zone is as shown below :

Ramachandrapuram	...	696.20 persons/sq mile
Medchal	...	631.91 "
Ghatkesar	...	604.68 "
Shamshabad	...	543.35 "

The highest residential built up area is in Ghatkesar followed by Shamshabad, Ramachandrapuram and Medchal. Ramachandrapuram is the leading industrial centre, when compared with the other three towns. The other three towns are comparatively less industrialised. Only Ghatkesar stands next to Ramachandrapuram in the number of industrial establishments. This may be due to the lack of any major basic industry, which can create impetus for industrial growth. However, the local planning authority is encouraging Andhra Pradesh Industrial Infrastructure Corporation Limited to take up industrial schemes for the growth of these towns.

NOTES

1. Development Plan of Hyderabad, 1975.
2. Master Plan of Delhi Prepared by DDA and Published in 1962.
3. Details from Master Plan of Delhi 1962 and National Capital Region prepared by TCPO.

5

GROWTH OF RAMACHANDRAPURAM-PATANCHERUVU

RAMACHANDRAPURAM is a small village in Sangareddy *taluk* of Medak district located at a distance of 25 km on the Hyderabad-Bombay highway from the Hyderabad city. The picture of the village till 1961, when BHEL township was not established, is briefly described below:

The area of the village is 3.50 sq miles. It was having a population of 921 with 479 males and 442 females in which 223 were illiterates. The number of houses were 149 with 160 households living in them. It was having one primary school. It had a *gram panchayat*.

The occupation structure in the village till 1961 was as shown in Table 5.1.

TABLE 5.1 : Occupational Structure in Ramachandrapuram Village, 1961

Total workers	*Cultivators*	*Agri labourers*	*Mining/ Quarying*	*Household*	*Manfufacturing*	*Construction*	*Transportation and Communication*	*Transport and Commerce*	*Others*
433	165	147	3	31	14	6	40	3	24
(100.0)	(38.11)	(33.95)	(0.69)	(7.16)	(3.23)	(1.39)	(9.24)	(0.69)	(5.5)

(*Source* : Medak district Census handbook 1961.)

The table shows that the dominant economic activity was agriculture up to 1961. Thus Ramachandrapuram was a humble village falling under the peripheral influence of Hyderabad metropolis till the year 1961.

Establishment of BHEL and ICRISAT

The decision to locate the BHEL, a large manufacturing industry, at Ramachandrapuram of Patancheruvu block of Sangareddy *taluk* in Medak district by the Government of India brought several changes not only in Ramachandrapuram village but also in the surrounding villages.

The Government of Andhra Pradesh acquired 2,317.4 hectares of agriculture and other lands covering the villages Kachireddipalle, Manmade, Tellapur, Ramachandrapuram and Patancheruvu for the purpose of the factory and the township exercising its powers of acquisition under Land Acquisition Act. Most of the agricultural land was acquired from these villages for the establishment of the factory. However, village sites were left as they were and BHEL did not have use of the entire land and limited itself to an area of 947.5 hectares for their immediate requirements but the compensation had been paid fully.[1]

The villagers whose land thus left unused continued to cultivate them and the Government did not raise any objection though they were told that they had to vacate the land eventually when needed. The double benefit enjoyed by the villages continued up to 1971, when the Government of India and Government of Andhra Pradesh decided to locate International Crops Research Institute for Semi-Arid Tropics (ICRISAT) in the same area.

The villages which were worst affected by this decision were Kachireddipalle and Manmde. Previously the agricultural land alone was acquired, but with the decision to locate ICRISAT, the village sites and the homesteads of the villagers were evaluated and compensation paid to the villagers to move out of the villages forever. The villagers were allowed to take the building materials of semi-permanent and temporary structures. The *pucca* buildings were left as it were for use to the new organisation in case they need. Thus the two villages were completely evacuated to serve the purpose of locating new major economic activity. The village site and some part of agricultural land of Ramachandrapuram is left as it is. So it is not the Ramachandrapuram village but the surrounding villages which were worst affected by the location of the large manufacturing industry and the international crops research institute.

Rehabilitation of the Displaced Villagers

The BHEL authorities agreed to part with 41.8 hectares of land for rehabilitating these villagers adjacent to their township. The area faiis under the jurisdiction of Ramachandrapuram *panchayat*.

When BHEL was being built in the early '60s, one of the contractors from Bombay brought some labourers and got them settled on the outskirts of the present BHEL complex. They continued to live there even after the construction was completed, but they were not permitted to build permanent structures. This habitat was called 'Bombay Bazaar' taking its name from the contractor who hailed from Bombay.[2]

The BHEL authorities wanted to part with some land originally allotted to them for shifting the people from Bombay Bazaar without any compensation. They also agreed to absorb the labour into the factory work. Thus all the residents of Kachireddipalle, Manmde and Bombay Bazaar were asked to shift to the new settlement, which shall be called as Ramachandrapuram new settlement because it comes under the administrative jurisdiction of the Ramachandrapuram *Gram Panchayat*.

The details of the villages Kachireddipalle, Manmole along with Bombay Bazaar are given below :

1. *Kachireddipalle*		
land acquired:	:	304.47 hectares
distance from Patancheruvu	:	2 km
Panchayat	:	Ramachandrapuram Panchayat
Nearest Town	:	Ramachandrapuram township
Total Population	:	815 Male - 416 Female - 399
No. of occupied residential houses	:	104
No. of households	:	130
Total No. of workers	:	270 Male - 210 Female - 60
Service facilities	:	Primary School
2. *Manmole*		
No. of lands acquired	:	1015.15 hectares
Distance from Patancheruvu	:	5 km
Panchayat	:	Panchayat was denotified in 1973 and merged with Ramachandrapuram

(Contd.)

(*Contd.*)

Nearest Town	:	Ramachandrapuram township
Total population	:	2664 Male - 1338 Female - 1326
No. of occupied residential houses	:	362
No. of households	:	479
Total No. of workers	:	1052 Male - 760 Female - 292
Service facilities	:	High School

3. *Bombay Bazaar*

It was established by the construction workers in an area adjacent to the BHEL factory complex :

Total population	:	777 Male - 394 Female - 383
No. of houses	:	177 (thatched roof with mud walls etc.,)
No. of households	:	192

(All the figures mentioned are as per 1971 Census).

Thus two groups of long established villagers and one group of recently settled industrial employees were brought together to live in physical proximity with one another in the new settlement. They have been allotted land plots for house construction varying in size depending upon their previous homestead in their respective former villages. Two types of plots have been allotted – 'A' of the size of 60′x40′ and 'B' of the size of 40′x30′. The location of Ramachandrapuram new settlement is as shown in Map 5.1.

The details of Ramachandrapuram new settlement are as given below :

- It stands between BHEL and ICRISAT and is about three km from Patancheruvu and almost within the vicinity of Ramachandrapuram village.
- It has an area of 4.17 hectares with 13.3 hectares residential area. The sites for the three villages has been clearly demarcated separately in the layout plan.

MAP 5.1 : Location of Ramachandrapuram New Settlement

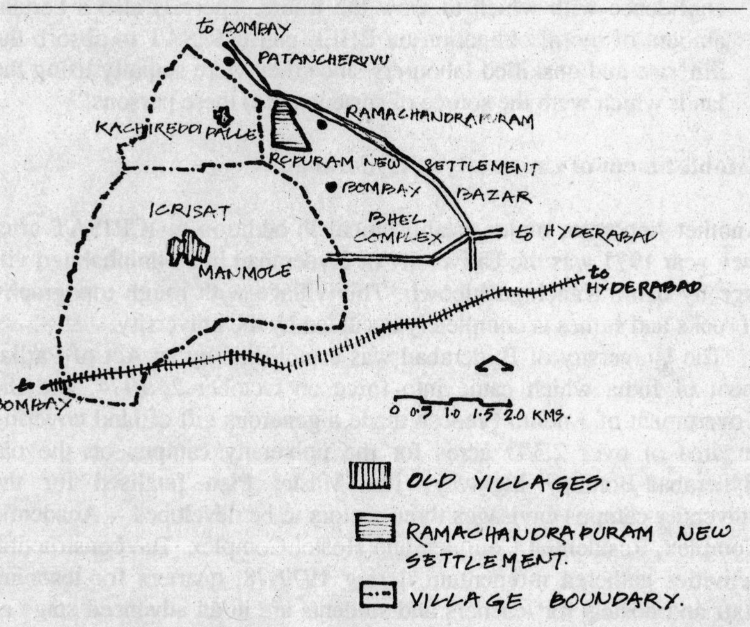

Source: Rehabilitation of Displaced Villagers — NIRD, Hyderabad

Sites for primary school, a temple, a mosque, a church, primary health centre, shops, parks, roads, burial grounds and also open spaces for future expansion are provided.

Kutcha roads had been provided connecting all the streets in the Ramachandrapuram new settlement. 12 borewells with hand-pumps were installed by the Government. Two open wells were dug by Ramachandrapuram *Panchayat*.

A recent survey by the Institute of Rural (then Community) Development at Hyderabad shows the anxiety of the residents about their future life and the problems in the adjustment of the villagers with different socio-cultural backgrounds. The report points out and suggests :

'The most crying need of the new settlement is to provide the uprooted people with a modicum of psychological re-assurance. The sense of deprivation could be reduced if sympathetic and qualified social workers were to inculcate amongst them a certain amount of confidence with which to view the future. There is also a certain amount of moral obligation on BHEL and ICRISAT to absorb the illiterate and unskilled labourers since they were actually using the lands which were the source of sustenance to these persons.'[3]

Establishment of University of Hyderabad

Another important major establishment in addition to ICRISAT after they year 1971 was the University of Hyderabad in an uninhabited village by name Kanchigachibowli. This village with rough topography of rocks and stones is completely occupied by the university.

The University of Hyderabad was established by an Act of Parliament of India which came into force on October 2, 1974, and the Government of Andhra Pradesh made a generous gift of land covering an area of over 2,300 acres for the university campus on the old Hyderabad-Bombay highway. The Master Plan finalised for the university campus envisages three sectors to be developed – Academic Complex, Residential Complex and Hostel Complex. The construction activities gathered momentum during 1977-78, quarters for teaching staff and hostels for teachers and students are in an advanced stage of progress.[4]

Thus, there are three major establishments in the Ramachandrapuram zone in the shape of BHEL, ICRISAT and University of Hyderabad. The BHEL complex was established around 1964 whereas the other two were established after 1971.

Industrial Development in Patancheruvu

The development of Patancheruvu as an industrial centre is mainly due to the establishment of Andhra Pradesh Industrial Infrastructure Corporation Ltd. Patancheruvu as a block headquarters fortunately falls within the administrative boundary of Medak district which entitles it for all Centre and State Government aids for development.

The picture of the village till 1971 was as follows :

- * Area of the village : 4.48 sq miles
- * Status : block headquarters (re-constitu-

ted in 1964 with the inclusion of Sadasivpet block)

*	Total population	:	4983 – Male - 2581 Female - 2402
*	Nearest town	:	Ramachandrapuram township
*	No. of occupied residential houses	:	703
*	No. of households	:	978
*	Total no. of workers	:	1788 – Male - 1377 Female - 411
*	Service facilities:		

Two *Zilla Parishad* high schools for boys and girls, a Samithi Central primary school, a Prevocational training centre, Rural health centre, Family and Child Welfare Centre, Workshops, a branch of State Bank of Hyderabad, Farmers Training Office, Cinema house, rice mill and telephone.

There is a need to know the functions of the Andhra Pradesh Industrial Infrastructure Corporation Ltd. to understand the Industrial development at Patancheruvu.

Functions[5]

- Identification of growth centres.
- Acquisition of land for industrial estates and industrial development areas.
- Establishment of industrial estates and industrial development areas, construction of sheds and formation of developed plots with infrastructure facilities like internal roads, water supply, power supply in the industrial estates and industrial development areas.
- Construction of houses for industrial workers near the industrial estates and industrial development areas.
- Sanction of bridge loans to the entrepreneurs to meet their short-term financial needs.
- Sanction of voluntary loan contributions to the A.P. State Electricity Board on behalf of the entrepreneurs for arranging power supply.
- Acting as an agent to the government in disbursing margin money, Central subsidy and State incentives.

– Co-ordination with government departments and other organisations to ensure transport, postal, telephone and other facilities in the industrial estates and industrial employment areas and credit facilities to the entrepreneurs.

What do they mean by Industrial Estates and Industrial Development areas?

– *Industrial Estates* : Industrial estates are dispersed in small places to meet the needs of small entrepreneurs. Factory sheds and smaller plots are developed and other facilities like internal roads, water, power, etc., are provided in these places. Example : ancillary industrial estates, autonagars and commercial complexes.
– *Industrial Development areas* : Industrial development areas are established for medium and major industries. Larger plots are developed, internal roads are laid and other facilities like water supply, power supply, drainage, etc., are provided in the industrial development areas.

In Patancheruvu both the industrial estates and industrial development areas are established. The housing scheme proposed by APIIC for the industrial workers with the help of HUDCO at Patancheruvu is given in Table 5.2.

TABLE 5.2 : Proposed Housing Scheme for Patancheruvu Village

		EWS	*LIG*	*MIG*	*Total*
Patancheruvu	I Phase	192	112	55	359
	II Phase	192	86	42	320

The allotment is on the basis of hire/purchase.

Patancheruvu is also eligible for 15 per cent Central Government subsidy investment. This scheme was launched with a view to remove the economic regional imbalances in certain notified parts of the country. Under this scheme, new industries and units taking up substantial expansion exceeding 10 per cent of the capital assets of the existing units are eligible for 15 per cent subsidy on the capital investment of the units up to a maximum limit of Rs.15 lakhs.

Patancheruvu being a block headquarters has got certain developed infrastructure and social service facilities. In addition to this its nearness to Ramachandrapuram and Hyderabad city enabled the prospective entrepreneurs to grab the incentives offered with both hands leading to a fast industrial growth in the area.

The growth so far in Ramachandrapuram zone is not deliberately planned in an integrated manner. Each organisation tried to make a place in the area with the help of the government policies, but the fact cannot be denied that all the three establishments favoured the location due to its nearness to Hyderabad city. Each decision or policy was made to satisfy a particular need rather than looking at the comprehensive development of the area. Thus the entire growth of Ramachandrapuram zone could be divided into three phases.

I. Upto 1961 when the whole zone was dominated by agriculture as a main economic activity.

II. After the establishment of BHEL and till 1971 when a major impetus for industrial growth was initiated, particularly in the villages around the BHEL township.

III. After 1971 establishment of ICRISAT and University of Hyderabad. Rehabilitation of villagers in the Ramachandrapuram new settlement. Identification of Patancheruva for industrial development by APIIC.

NOTES

1. Muthayya B.S. and Mathur T.S. (1975). ***Rehabilitation of displaced Villagers***, National Institute of Community Development, Hyderabad.
2. *Ibid.*
3. *Ibid.*
4. University of Hyderabad — General Information for Admission, 1980-81.
5. 'APIIC — A catalyst for Industrial Growth in Andhra Pradesh' — a Pamphlet.

6

REGIONAL INFLUENCE OF RAMACHANDRAPURAM

WHENEVER A major basic industry is introduced in a new area, it is bound to influence the surrounding region under normal circumstances. The BHEL factory which was established around the year 1964 at Ramachandrapuram village in Medak district with a planned township should have influenced certain area around the factory and the township. The influence region of Ramachandrapuram township should be viewed under two aspects :

1. The factory as well as the township's proximity to the metropolitan Hyderabad city, which being a bigger magnet likely to attract much larger region for various reasons, and the delimited metropolitan region was explained in the earlier chapter.
2. Even though Ramachandrapuram township falls under the shadow of Hyderabad metropolitan region, it should have influenced an area surrounding it similar to a small town serving as a service centre in spite of being a part of a bigger metropolitan area.

The area of influence is another important factor which needs careful consideration. The metropolitan city could influence much larger region because of its well-developed commercial activities and established transportation network. The same may not be possible in the case of Ramachandrapuram, which is a new township and the transportation network is not as good as the metropolis except the highway, which bypasses the township. Thus the town is likely to influence much smaller area which can be a part of the metropolitan region.

In a study of regional development in South and South-East Asia, sponsored by the United Nations Research Institute for Social Development, the authors pointed out :

> "In spite of the agglomeration forces the geographical dispersal of industrial development is, rightly or wrongly, accepted almost everywhere in the region as a desirable social objective."[1]

Now, accepting that Ramachandrapuram was built to serve a social objective either knowingly or unkowingly by the mentors, the influence region of Ramachandrapuram could be de-limited tentatively.

De-limitation of the Influence Region

The main aim in showing the tentative influence region of Ramachandrapuram is to confirm the assumption that the surrounding villages had considerable impact with the establishment of the factory and it acts as a work centre for the surrounding villages.

To find out the tentative influence region, the nearness and accessibility of the town has been taken as a criteria for de-limiting. This could be open to criticism, but it has been accepted in theory in the present case that the nearness to the town will play a vital role in influencing the village economy. It was proved in several cases earlier that the nearness to an urban centre affects the village economy.

Now with the help of district census reports, all the villages which have Ramachandrapuram township of BHEL factory as the nearest town has been taken into consideration to de-limit the influence region. The average distance observed is eight km from the village to the township.

There are 35 villages for whom Ramachandrapuram serves as the nearest town, in which Serinalagandla and Rendlagadda are uninhabted villages as per 1971 Census. The Ramachandrapuram zone of the Hyderabad Development Area marked by the local Hyderabad Urban Development Authority consists of 23 villages. Seventeen villages from the Ramachandrapuram zone are included in the tentative influence region along with 18 villages of Sangaraddy *taluk*, Medak district. Thus the de-limited influence region comprises 17 villages of Hyderabad west *taluk* and eighteen villages of Sangareddy *taluk* Map No. 6.1.

MAP 6.1 : Influence Region of Ramachandrapuram

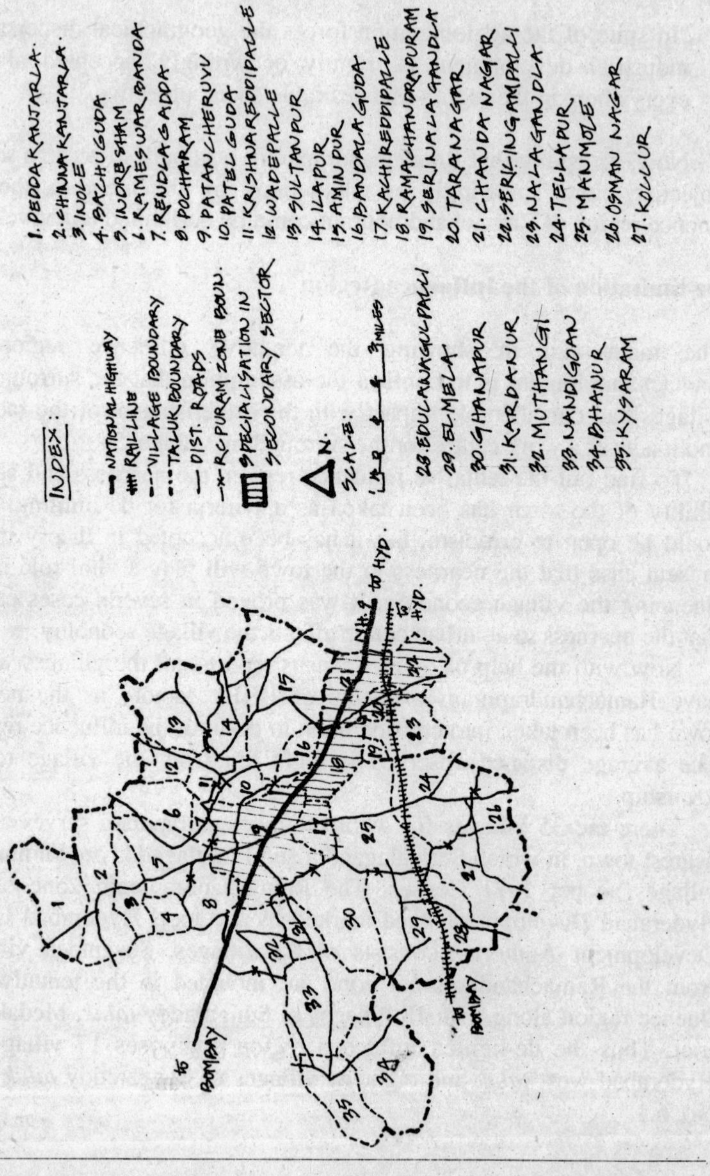

Source: Central Survey Office & HUDA, Hyderabad

Changes in the Occupation Structure

The next step is to find out the influence cast by the BHEL factory since its establishment around 1964 at Ramachandrapuram. To establish the changes the following factors were considered.

The occupation structure in the region before the establishment of the factory and after the establishment of the factory could show the power of Ramachandrapuram as a regional employment centre. To find out the changes, the occupation structure of the years 1961 and 1971 were compared with the help of census reports.

TABLE 6.1 : Occupational Structure in the Influence Region 1961 and 1971

	1961	*1971*	*Growth Rate*
Total workers	15,910	17,475	9.8
Primary	12,801	12,820	0.15
Secondary	1,550	2,340	50.00
Tertiary	1,502	2,277	51.60

(*Source* : District Census Handbook 1961-1971 Hyderabad and Medak.)

From Table 6.1 it is evident that the increase in the number of workers in total in 1971 is mainly due to the increase in the number of workers in secondary and tertiary sectors. The tertiary sector growth rate depends mainly on the development of the secondary sector, so the secondary sector can be taken as the major activity which increased the total number of workers.

Another important observation is that the tertiary sector should develop at a faster growth rate when there is a significant increase in the secondary sector, but the table shows that the growth rates of both the sectors are almost the same. This leads to an inference that the tertiary sector did not develop to the required level as a supporting activity.

The primary sector is almost stagnant in between the decade 1961 and 1971. It is a general opinion that whenever a new major activity tries to make its place, it will definitely cast influence on the major activity already prevalent. In the present situation, the major activity is the primary sector, but a new major activity in the shape of secondary sector emerged as a force by the year 1971 making the growth of primary sector almost stagnant. This leads to a conclusion that workers would have taken to primary activity if secondary activity is not available as a major activity. Since secondary sector emerged as a force by 1971, the primary sector felt the impact and the number of workers in this particular sector were almost stagnant between the decade 1961-71. It means few workers took the primary sector jobs in preference to the secondary sector jobs resulting in the stagnancy of the primary sector workers. This could be further substantiated with the help of the following Table 6.2.

TABLE 6.2 : Percentage Share of each Sector in the Region 1961-71

Year	*Item*	*Primary*	*Secondary*	*Tertiary*	*Total*
1961	No. of workers	12,801	1,550	1,502	15,910
	Percentage share of total workers	80.5	9.7	9.4	100
1971	No. of workers	12,820	2,340	2,277	17,475
	Percentage share of total workers	73.6	13.4	13.0	100

(*Source* : District Census Handbook 1961-1971 Hyderabad and Medak.)

From Table 6.2 it is apparent that the percentage share of primary sector to the total workers went down nearly 7.5 per cent between the years 1961 and 1971, and also the percentage share of secondary and tertiary sectors increased by nearly 4.0 per cent between 1961 and 1971. The increase in the share of workers by the secondary sector helped the tertiary sector also to increase its percentage share of total workers. Thus, it appears that tertiary sector is directly dependent on the growth of secondary sector workers.

The earlier Table 6.1 showed the stagnant growth rate of primary sector between 1961-71 years and the present Table 6.2 shows the decrease in the percentage share of total workers by the primary sector, which leads to the inference that the secondary sector, particularly the establishment of new industries, led to the stagnant growth rate and decrease in the percentage share of the primary sector. The above statistical evidence emphasises that the establishment of major basic activity in the shape of BHEL factory at Ramachandrapuram created a spurt for industrial growth which ultimately influenced the existing occupation pattern in the region.

To extend the argument further and find out the relative development of other sectors in relation to secondary sector, the relative index numbers method can be helpful.

One type of index numbers is structural numbers obtained by relating the whole population to 1, or more frequently to 100 or 1,000 (or some larger power of ten).

Table 6.3 shows the secondary sector as the base number and other components are related to it to find out the changes in the occupation structure between 1961-71:

TABLE 6.3 : Occupational Structure of each Sector between 1961-1971

Sector	*1961*	*1971*
Primary	825.8	547.8
Secondary	100.0	100.0
Tertiary	100.0	97.3

(*Source* : District Census Handbook 1961-71 Hyderabad & Medak.)

The base number for the secondary sector is denoted by 100. In relation to this sector, the primary sector constituted 825.8 per cent in 1961 and dropped to 547.8 per cent in 1971 showing a decrease of 278 per cent between the decade 1961-71. This further throws light on the emergence of secondary sector as a force reducing the share of primary sector considerably. On the other hand, tertiary sector had a share of 100 per cent in 1961 but it decreased to 97.3 per cent showing a fall of 2.7 per cent in the decade. This fall reveals the fact that the tertiary sector did not grow with the secondary sector and it is less than secondary sector growth. It leads to a conclusion that the tertiary sector did not develop to the desired level as expressed earlier.

Spatial Distribution of the Economic Activities

The next step is to know the spatial distribution of primary, secondary and tertiary activities to find their concentration or diversification over the entire region.

Gini co-efficient is the best known measure of diversification or concentration and it is based on the spatial Lorenz Curve.

A brief description about the construction of the Lorenz Curve would be useful to understand the inferences. First, the total workers and the total workers in the primary, secondary and tertiary sectors were tabulated for each village. The percentage share of each village in the total workers of the region and in the total workers of the primary, secondary and tertiary sectors of the region was calculated. Then the 'R' value for each village was found.

The 'R' value was obtained by dividing the percentage share of a particular sector with the percentage share of the total workers (Table 6.4).

TABLE 6.4 : Finding 'R' Value

	Total workers (Percentage)	*Primary sector (Percentage)*	*R value (Percentage)*	*Secondary sector (Percentage)*	*R value (Percentage)*	*Tertiary sector (Percentage)*	*R Value (Percentage)*
Ramachandrapuram	2.7	2.5	0.9	2.9	1.1	4.5	1.6

Thus the 'R' value of each village for each sector, viz., primary, secondary and tertiary, was found. Then the 'Rs' were arranged in a descending order for each sector like 0.5, 0.4, 0.3, ...

According to the descending order of the 'R' values the cumulative percentages were found for each sector along with the cumulative percentages of the total workers (Table 6.5).

TABLE 6.5 : Cumulative percentages of total workers and each sector

(Percentages)

Total workers	*Cumulative*	*Primary sector*	*Cumulative*	*R Value*
0.7	0.7	0.9	0.9	1.3
1.8	2.5	2.4	3.3	1.2
2.3	4.8	2.7	6.0	1.1

Thus the cumulative percentages for all the sectors, along with the cumulative percentages of the total, were found.

These cumulative percentages were plotted on a graph with the cumulative percentage of the total workers on X-axis and the cumulative percentage of the sectoral workers on the Y-axis separately for primary, secondary and tertiary sectors for the years 1961 and 1971. The curves obtained are shown in 6.1, 6.2 & 6.3.

If the curve is closer to the diagonal, the spread of employment is even over the industrial categories. if the curve is farther from the diagonal it indicates diversification in the industrial categories. The gini co-efficient is defined as the ratio A/A+B.

GRAPH 6.1 : Cumulative percentage of the total workers

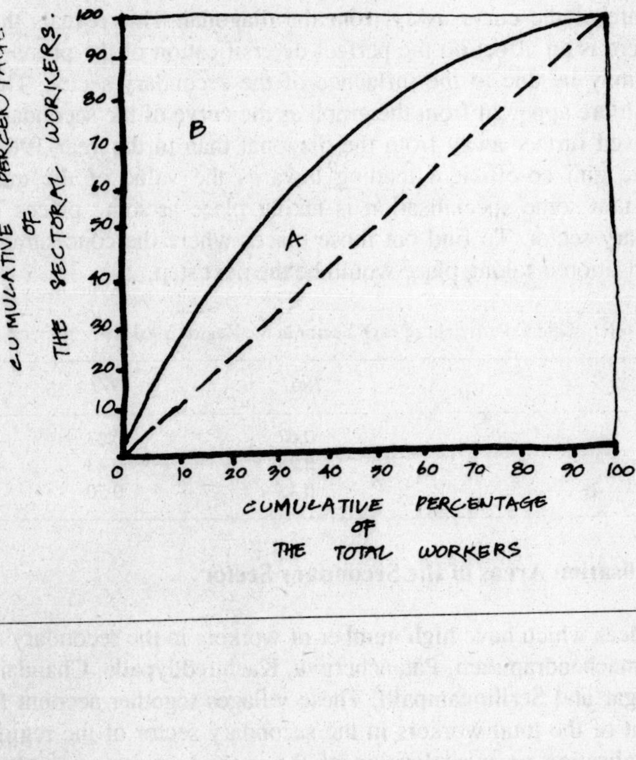

It has extreme values of zero (perfect diversification) and of unity (perfect specialisation). The value in-between these two can be judged based on its inclination either to zero or to unity.

The Lorenz Curve for the primary, secondary and tertiary sectors in the influence region is as shown in the graphs for 1961 and 1971 years. The gini co-efficient of the same sectors for the years 1961 and 1971 is shown in Table 6 6.

From the Table 6.6 it is evident that the employment in the primary sector was almost evenly distributed or near to perfect diversification in the year 1961, but in the year 1971 there is a change showing the departure of the curve away from the diagonal. This reveals the fact that there is an affect on the perfect diversification of the primary sector. It may be due to the influence of the secondary sector. This becomes more apparent from the graph as the curve of the secondary sector moved further away from the diagonal than in the year 1961, and also the gini co-efficient tending towards the value of the unity. It shows that some specialisation is taking place at some places in the secondary sector. To find out those places where the concentration or specialisation is taking place would be the next step.

TABLE 6.6 : Gini Co-efficient of each Sector in the Region 1961-71

	1961	*1971*
Primary	0.07	0.23
Secondary	0.28	0.43
Tertiary	0.43	0.50

Specialisation Areas of the Secondary Sector

The places which have high number of workers in the secondary sector are Ramachandrapuram, Patancheruvu, Kachireddypalle, Chandanagar, Taranagar and Serilingampalli. These villages together account for 52 per cent of the total workers in the secondary sector of the region. So the localisation or specialisation of the secondary sector as observed from Table 6.4 could be taking place in these villages.

To carry the argument further and to establish the assumption that the specialisation is taking place in Ramachandrapuram, Patancheruvu, Kachireddipalle, Chandanagar, Taranagar and Serilingampalli, the location quotient is a good measure to use.

The location quotient is a measure of relative importance of a given economic activity or group of activities. It helps in comparing different places on the basis of the specialisation of economic activities. If the location quotient value is unity or less than unity it means no specialisation and greater the location quotient over the unity, greater the specialisation of the activity.

The location quotient for each village was found based on the following formula :[2]

GRAPH 6.2 : Spatial Lorenz Curve for Primary, Secondary and Tertiary Sectors year 1961

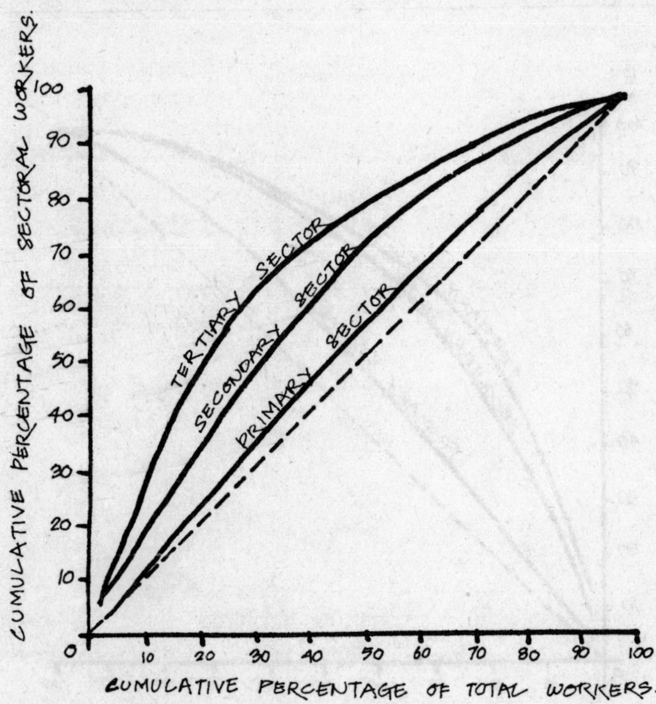

$$\text{Location quotient} = \frac{Si/Ni}{S/N}$$

Si = No. of wage earners in an industry in a given region
S = No. of wage earners in all industries in a given region (village named)
Ni = No. of wage earners in an industry in the State (the influence region)
N = No. of wage earners in all industries in the State.

The individual location quotients for all the six villages were found for the years 1961 and 1971 and their values are as shown in Table 6.7.

GRAPH 6.3 : Spatial Lorenz Curve for Primary, Secondary and Tertiary Sectors Year 1971

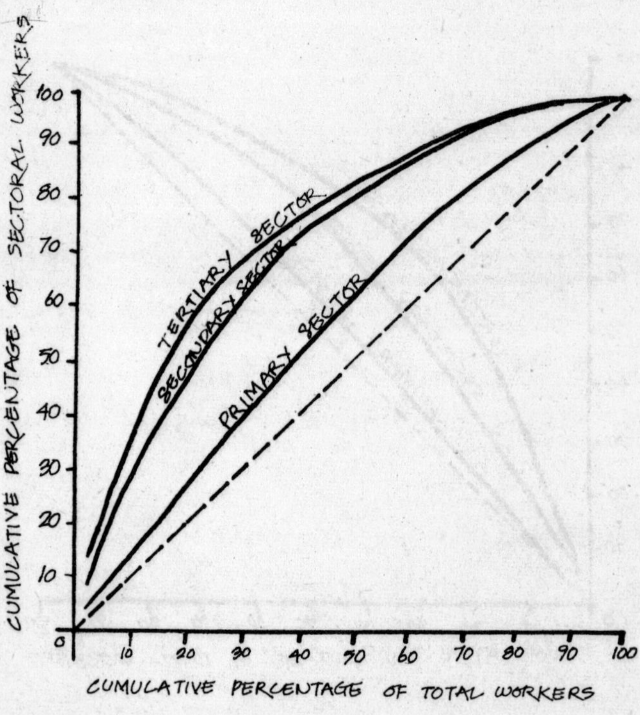

TABLE 6.7 : Location Quotient of the specialisation areas 1961-71

		1961	*1971*
Ramachandrapuram	...	1	2.3
Kachireddipalle	...	1	2.5
Patancheruvu	...	1	1.5
Chandanagar	...	0.3	2.0
Taranagar	...	1.0	3.5
Serilingampalli	...	1.5	2.5

From the Table 6.7 it is evident that none of the villages had any kind of specialisation in the secondary sector, but by 1971 all the villages show values above the unity, indicating specialisation of the secondary sector. The main reason for this kind of localisation of the secondary sector is due to the establishment of BHEL factory at Ramachandrapuram, and the growth of ancillary industries around the factory. So these villages show high degree of specialisation in the secondary sector when compared with the other villages in the influence region. Thus the specialisation areas as marked on the Map 6.1 include the township, Ramachandrapuram, Kachireddipalle Patancheruvu, Chandanagar, Taranagar and Serilingampalli.

NOTES

1. Quoted in Ashish Bose (1978). *India's Urbanisation (1901-2001)*, Tata McGraw-Hill Publishing Company, New Delhi.
2. Adopted from Manzoor Alam (1969), "*The Hyderabad Metropolitan Research Project*" — Prepared by Osmania University and Institute of Asian Studies, Hyderabad (Mimeographed).

7

DEMOGRAPHIC CHARACTERISTICS OF RAMACHANDRAPURAM ZONE

THERE SHOULD be an areal unit for planning the town. Though the boundary of the town could be arbitrary, the area taken for planning should be sufficiently big and comprehensive for planning purpose. The influence region is too big an area for planning the nucleus town. The purpose of the present study is confined to the town plan, so the Ramachandrapuram zone as delineated by Hyderabad Urban Development Authority for Planning purpose has been taken as an areal unit for planning (Map 7.1).

Economic participation rate is a measure to know the degree of utilisation of manpower resources and it is defined as number of persons working per hundred population. There is enough evidence to show that in India the economic participation rates are higher where there is concentration of primary activities than in the urban areas.

Economic participation rate for both Ramachandrapuram zone and the influence region was found to give a comparative picture. Its value in Ramachandrapuram zone is 28.9 per cent and 43.5 per cent in the influence region. The low rate in Ramachandrapuram zone is apparently due to the concentration of secondary activities. Thus, it is obvious that this areal unit is picking up secondary and tertiary activities displacing primary activities.

Density and Growth of Population

The variations in the density of population of each village at the regional level is a good measure to understand the growth trends of population and the concentration of population.

MAP 7.1 : Ramachandrapuram — Patancheruvu Zone

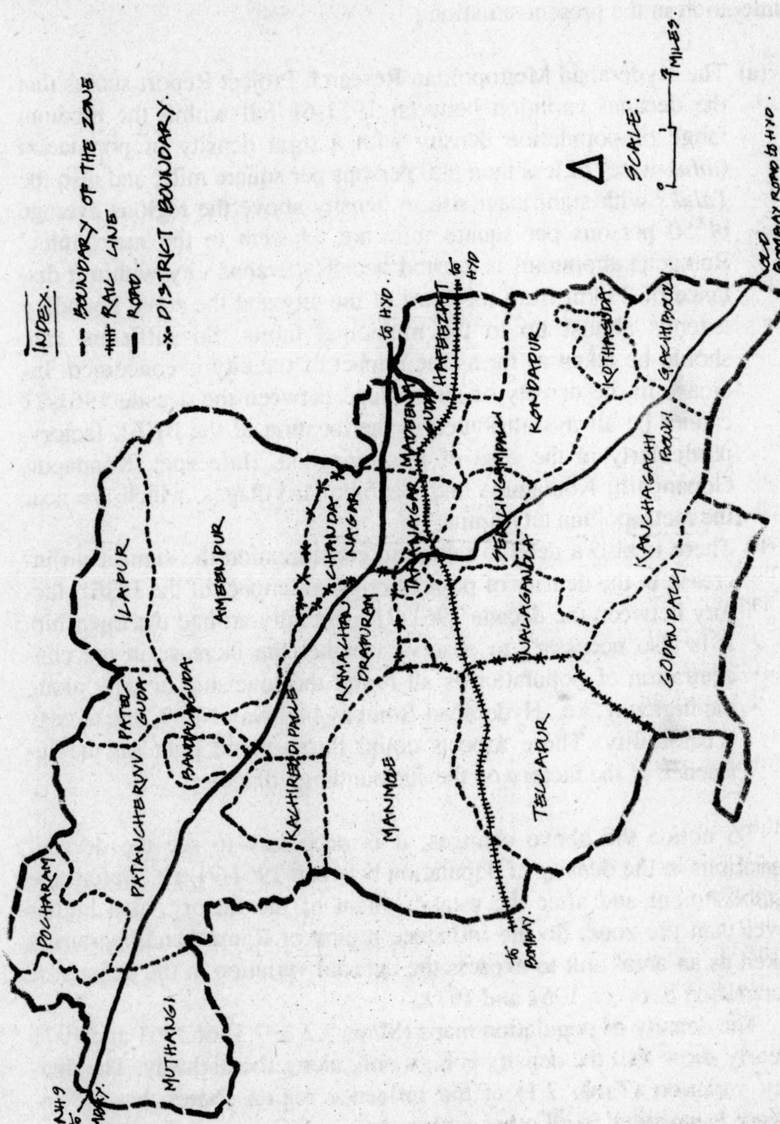

Source: H.U.D.A., Hyderabad

There are two important aspects which should be taken into consideration in the present situation :

(a) The Hyderabad Metropolitan Research Project Report shows that the decadal variation between 1951-61 fell within the medium range of population density with a rural density of population (*taluk*-wise) of less than 500 persons per square mile, and also the *Taluks* with significant rise in density above the regions average of 50 persons per square mile are adjacent to the metropolis.[1] Ramachandrapuram is located near Hyderabad city within a distance of 25 km from the heart of the city and the zonal boundary extends almost up to the municipal limits. So sufficient care should be taken as far as the impact of the city is concerned. Increase in the density of any village between the decade 1961-71 cannot be always attributed to the location of the BHEL factory, particularly in the case of Madeenaguda, Hafeezpet, Kondapur, Gopanpalli, Kothaguda and Gachibowli villages, which are near the metropolitan city limits.

(b) There is also a need to take into consideration the significant increase in the density of population as an impact of the BHEL factory between the decade 1961-71 especially around the township. It is also necessary to observe whether the increase in the concentration of population is all round the township or only along the highway, i.e., Hyderabad-Bombay highway No. 9, due to easy accessibility. These aspects could throw some light on the influence of the factory on the surrounding villages.

To notice the above changes, it is necessary to see the decadal variations in the density of population between 1961-71, i.e., before the establishment and after the establishment of the factory, at a higher level than the zone. So the influence region of Ramachandrapuram is taken as an areal unit to express the decadal variation in the density of population between 1961 and 1971.

The density of population maps (Maps 7.2 & 7.3) of 1961 and 1971 clearly show that the density is high only along the highway. The density variation (Table 7.1) of the influence region shows that the increase is marginal in all other settlements.

The villages which got re-densified showing comparatively high rate of increase in the density of population are Ramachandrapuram, Patelguda, Kachireddipalle, Patancheruvu, Nalagandla, Serilingampalli, Taranagar and Chandanagar. Among these villages significant increase is registered by Taranagar, which started emerging as a nodal service centre for the surrounding villages. Though its nearness to Hyderabad city is true, but its high rate of population density could be attributed to the establishment of the factory and its convenient access to the surrounding villages.

MAP 7.2 : Ramachandrapuram Influence Region — Density of Population 1961 (No. of Persons Per Acre)

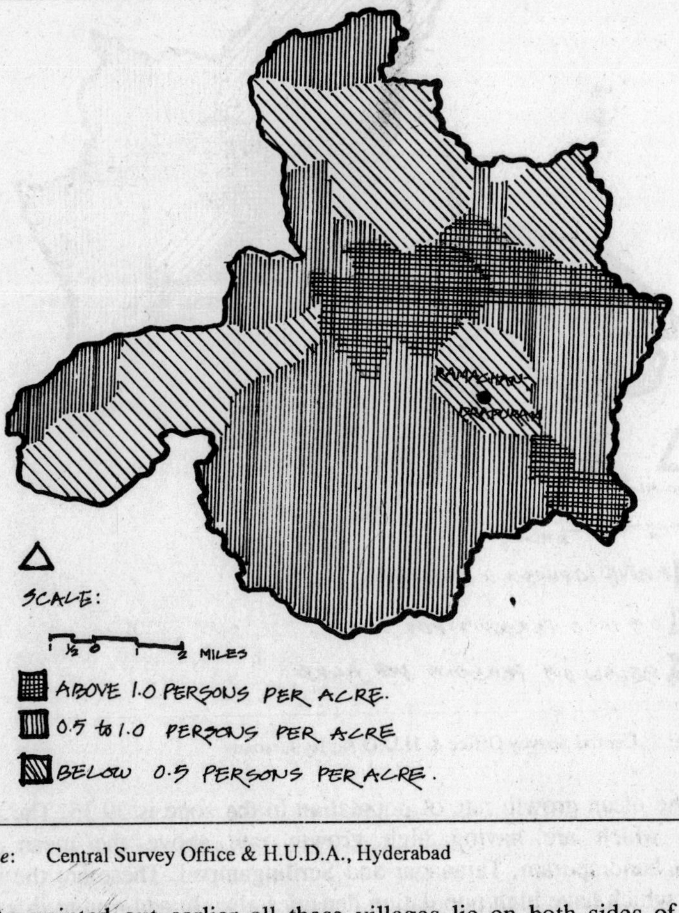

Source: Central Survey Office & H.U.D.A., Hyderabad

As pointed out earlier all these villages lie on both sides of the highway registered not only high population density but also got workers who are predominantly engaged in secondary and tertiary sector activities. This was shown in the earlier chapter with the help of location quotient while analysing the influence region of Ramachandrapuram.

MAP 7.3 : Ramachandrapuram Influence Region — Density of Population 1971 (No. of Persons Per Acre)

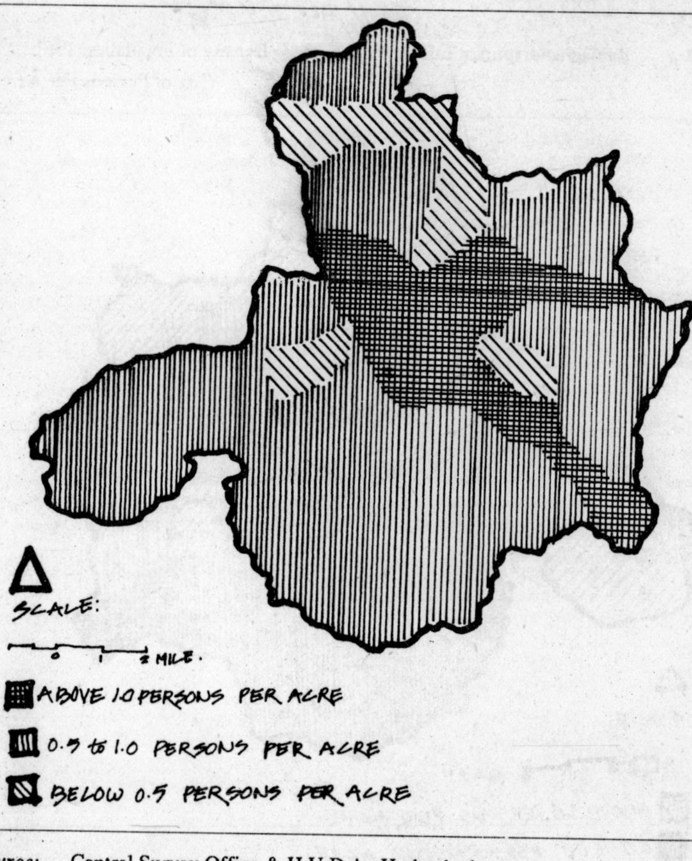

Source: Central Survey Office & H.U.D.A., Hyderabad

The mean growth rate of population in the zone is 39.35. The villages which are having high growth rate above the mean are Ramachandrapuram, Taranagar and Serilingampall. These are the villages which have high population densities also. In addition to this the creation of new BHEL township with a population of 11,146 is a completely new addition to the existing population, which created an impetus for industrial growth simultaneously resulting in the growth of population.

TABLE 7.1 : Variation in Population Density in the Influence Region of Ramachandrapuram

Village Name	*Density (Persons per acre)*		*Variation in Density*
	1961	*1971*	
Chinna Kanjarla	0.31	0.39	0.08
Pedda Kanjarla	0.82	1.00	0.18
Kysaram	0.60	0.80	0.20
Bhanur	0.45	0.54	0.09
Nandigaon	0.41	0.50	0.09
Inde	0.42	0.50	0.08
Bachuguda	0.60	0.80	0.20
Indresham	0.39	0.51	0.12
Wadakpalle	0.83	0.85	0.02
Sultanapur	0.38	0.52	0.14
Ilapur	1.83	3.33	1.50
Aminpur	0.53	0.68	0.15
Ramachandrapuram (Rural)	0.41	0.73	0.32
Bandalaguda	0.27	0.43	0.16
Patelguda	0.91	1.29	0.38
Krishnareddipalle	1.10	1.35	0.25
Rameswarbanda	0.16	0.24	0.08
Patancheruvu	1.27	1.74	0.47
Pocharam	0.96	1.16	0.20
Muthangi	0.60	0.74	0.14
Kardanur	0.39	0.47	0.08
Ghanapur	0.63	0.74	0.11
Manmole	0.57	0.77	0.20
Elmela	0.59	0.63	0.04
Edulanagulpalle	0.70	0.82	0.12
Kollur	0.39	0.54	0.15
Tellapur	0.63	0.84	0.21
Osman Nagar	0.51	0.66	0.15
Nalagandla	0.50	0.73	0.23
Serilingampalli	1.16	2.39	1.23
Taranagar	5.10	13.55	8.45
Chandanagar	0.52	0.94	0.42

(*Source : Distt. Census Handbook*, Hyderabad & Medak, 1961-1971.)

Another aspect is that high population growth rates above the mean growth rate of population are found not in the villages near the Hyderabad city but in the villages surrounding the Ramachandrapuram, BHEL township (Table 7.2). This further shows the impact of industrial growth and consequent increase in the growth rate of population. The significant increase in the growth rate of population in the villages could be due to migration (Table 7.3).

The immigrant component of population under the present circumstances could be based on two assumptions :[2]

1. The proportion by which the growth rate of a settlement exceeds the mean growth rate of the State (1961-71) represents the immigrant components of the population of that settlement.
2. The margin by which a rural settlement's growth exceeds the mean growth rate of the rural population of its own district will comprise the immigrant component of that settlement population.

TABLE 7.2 : Population Density in Ramachandrapuram Zone, 1961-71

Village Name	*Year 1961*	*Year 1971*	*Variation in Density*
Pocharam	0.96	1.16	0.20
Muthangi	0.60	0.74	0.14
Patancheruvu	1.27	1.74	0.47
Patelguda	0.91	1.29	0.38
Ilapur	1.83	3.33	1.50
Bandalaguda	0.27	0.43	0.16
Kachireddipalle	—	—	—
Manmole	0.57	0.77	0.20
Ramachandrapuram (Rural)	0.41	0.73	0.32
BHEL Township	—	4.98	4.98
Aminpur	0.53	0.68	0.15
Chandanagar	0.52	0.94	0.42
Taranagar	5.10	13.55	8.45
Madeenaguda	0.18	0.19	0.01
Hafeezpet	0.61	0.69	0.08
Tellapur	0.63	0.84	0.21
Nalagandla	0.50	0.73	0.23
Serilingampalli	1.16	2.39	1.23
Kondapur	0.25	0.26	0.01
Gopanpalli	0.42	0.42	0.00
Kothaguda	1.17	1.38	0.21
Gachibowli	0.06	0.08	0.02
Mean	0.90	1.78	0.92

(*Source: Distt. Census Handbook.* Hyderabad & Medak, 1961-1971).

TABLE 7.3 : Population Distribution in Ramachandrapuram Zone, 1961-71

Village Name	*1961*			*1971*		
	Total	*Male*	*Female*	*Total*	*Male*	*Female*
Pocharam	659	338	321	795 (+20.6)	424 (+25.44)	371 (+15.58)
Muthangi	1,188	569	619	1,474 (+24.0)	723 (+27.07)	751 (+21.32)
Patancheruvu	3,637	1,855	1,782	4,983 (+37.0)	2,581 (+39.14)	2,402 (+34.79)
Patelguda	273	131	142	387 (+41.8)	199 (+51.91)	188 (+32.39)
Ilapur	211	106	105	383 (+81.5)	197 (+85.45)	186 (+77.14)
Bandalaguda	278	138	140	449 (+61.5)	228 (+90.00)	221 (+36.65)
Kachireddipalle	624	315	309	815 (+30.6)	416 (+101.00)	339 (+29.13)
Manmole	1,987	988	999	2,664 (+34.0)	1,338 (+40.49)	1,326 (+32.73)
Ramachandrapuram (Rural)	921	479	442	1,646 (+78.7)	837 (+74.74)	809 (+83.03)
BHEL Township	—	—	—	11,146 (—)	5,783 (—)	5,363 (—)
Aminpur	1,507	771	736	1,957 (+29.9)	1,000 (+29.70)	957 (+30.03)
Chandanagar	660	328	332	1,207 (+82.9)	611 (+86.28)	596 (+79.52)
Taranagar	419	195	224	1,125 (+168.5)	593 (+204.10)	532 (+137.50)
Madeenaguda	179	92	87	189 (+5.59)	87 (-5.43)	102 (+17.24)
Hafeezpet	806	415	391	913 (+13.28)	463 (+11.57)	450 (+15.09)
Tellapur	2,009	1,001	1,008	2,683 (+33.5)	1,339 (+33.77)	1,344 (+33.34)
Nalagandla	730	348	382	1,080 (+48.0)	521 (+49.71)	559 (+46.34)
Serilingampalli	830	422	408	1,715 (+106.6)	939 (+122.51)	776 (+90.20)
Kondapur	553	306	247	563 (+1.81)	293 (-4.25)	270 (+9.31)
Gopanpalli	1,045	537	508	1,029 (-1.53)	512 (-4.66)	517 (+1.77)
Kothaguda	470	238	232	556 (+18.30)	296 (+24.37)	260 (+12.07)
Gachibowli	276	139	137	344 (+24.64)	166 (+19.42)	178 (+29.93)
Mean	19,262	9,711	9,551	38,103 (+97.81)	19,546 (+101.28)	18,557 (+94.29)

(*Source:* *Distt. Census Handbook.* Hyderabad & Medak, 1961-1971).
Note: Figures in bracket show the percentage of growth rate.

The individual growth rates of each village are given in the table 7.3. The immigrant component further fortifies the argument that Ramachandrapuram town serves as a regional employment centre

(Table 7.4). The influence region was shown earlier and the population is likely to move from these villages. Here the migrants cannot be regular commuters as in the case of a city because of the absence of well-developed transportation network. They would like to flock around the work centres. Thus, we find specialisation of industrial activity only around the basic industry where the people would like to concentrate.

Sex Ratio

There is one more indicator which shows the migrationary trends of the population. It is the sex ratio prevailing and the past.

In India, unlike in many of the industrially advanced Western countries, on account of the prevailing social and economic conditions, low sex ratio (expressed as number of females per 1,000 males) is considered as a good index, except in southern cities of urbanisation. The lower sex ratios could be interpreted to mean an influx of male inmigrants into such settlements.

A comparative picture of the sex ratios in relation to Hyderabad metropolitan area and Andhra Pradesh State is shown in Table 7.5.

TABLE 7.4: Comparative Mean Growth Rates of Rural Population 1971.

Ramachandrapuram Zone	*Andhra Pradesh State*	*Hyderabad District*	*Medak District*
+ 39.95	+ 18.15	+ 22.09	+ 18.59

(*Sources : District Census Handbook of Hyderabad & Medak* — Handbook of Statistics, Andhra Pradesh, 1979-80).

TABLE 7.5 : Comparative Sex Ratio, 1961-71

	1961	*1971*
Ramachandrapuram Zone	983	949
Hyderabad Metropolitan region	985	980
Andhra Pradesh	981	977

(*Source : District Census Handbook*, Hyderabad and Medak, Hyderabad Metropolitan Region Report, Handbook of Statistics, A.P., 1979-80).

A close observation at Table 7.5 shows that the sex ratios have fallen in general from 1961 to 1971 in all the three cases, but the sex ratio in Ramachandrapuram zone is much lower than the Hyderabad metropolitan region (Table 7.6).

It is better to have a look at the sex ratios at a higher level to know the trends. So the influence region is once again chosen as an areal unit to show the spatial variation in the sex ratios for 1971.

Map 7.4 clearly shows that the low sex ratios are in the villages along the highway. The villages which have higher sex ratios are further away indicating the industrial migration. This is a simple expression to understand the migration component in the growing population, but it is not the sole criterion for declining sex ratio which depend on many other factors, like, birth rate, death rate, fertility rate, etc.

TABLE 7.6 : Sex Ratio in Ramachandrapuram Zone, 1961-71

Village Name	*Year*	
	1961	*1971*
Pocharam	949	875
Muthangi	1,087	1,038
Patancheruvu	960	930
Patelguda	1,083	944
Ilapur	990	944
Bandalaguda	1,014	969
Kachireddipalle	981	959
Mamnole	1,011	991
Ramachandrapuram (Rural)	922	966
BHEL Township	—	927
Aminpur	954	957
Chandanagar	1,012	975
Taranagar	1,148	897
Madeenaguda	945	1,171
Hafeezpet	941	972
Tellapur	1,007	1,003
Nalagandla	1,097	1,073
Serilingampalli	967	826
Kondapur	807	921
Gopanpalli	946	1,009
Kothaguda	975	878
Gachibowli	985	1,072
Mean	989	968

(*Source: Distt. Census Handbook.* Hyderabad & Medak 1961-71.)

MAP 7.4 : Ramachandrapuram Influence Region Sex Ratio 1971

(No. of Females Per 1000 Males)

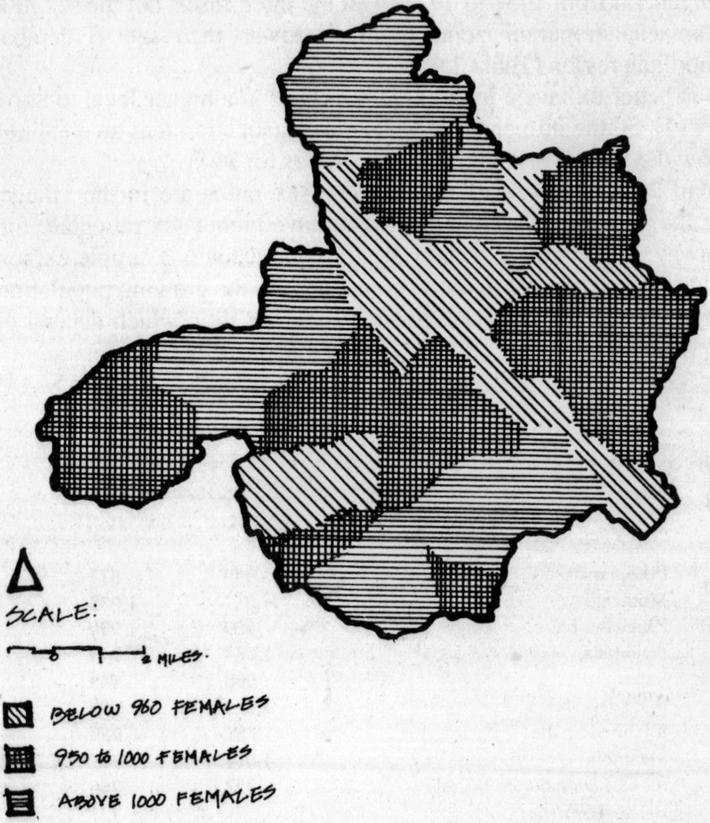

Source: Central Survey Office & H.U.D.A., Hyderabad

The declining sex ratio could be interpreted in several other ways, also, which show the migration trends. The increasing participation rate of male workers could be a reason for the declining female population in the zone. The female participation rate reduced considerably when compared to the male participation rate and there is an overall decline in the total participation rate of the population (Table 7.9 & 7.10). Since the decline is considerable, it could be taken as an attribute for the decrease in the sex ratio. This cannot be taken as an important criteria for the decline in the sex ratio because the definition of worker was polished and made more precise in 1971 Census than in 1961 Census, which caused a reduction in the total number of workers everywhere (Table 7.6).

The Graph 7.1 showing the percentage share of male workers and female workers out of the total workers gives an idea on the declining number of female workers. This is further supported by the graph showing the increasing number of dependents per worker between the decade 1961-71.

This leads to an inference that the declining sex ratio could be due to the declining female share of workers and the increasing share of male workers. When the male share of workers are dominant and the dependents per worker are increasing, it shows that the male workers must have moved with their families for employment. The number of such male workers are more than the female workers. Even in the migrant component for employment the male number should have been dominant, because if the female number is more then the number of dependents would have been less. The whole expression could be put in a simplified manner as below :

* increase in the the no. of dependents	decrease in the percentage share of female workers
* decrease in the percentage share of female workers	increase in the percentage share of male workers
* increase in the percentage share of male workers	increase in the number of male workers
* increase in the number of male workers	increase in the number of total male population
* increase in the total male population	increase in the total population
* increase in the total population due to male population	lowering sex ratio

There is no significant change in the average household size (Table 7.7) of the area. This indicates that other population characteristics did not have any empact on the average household size.

Another intresting fact is the decline in the male population in those villages which are near the metropolitan city limits. Madeenaguda, Kondapur and Gopanpalli show decreasing male population, which could be due to the migration of male workers to the city for employment. Since the villages are near the city limits, the metropolitan pull for employment is more than Ramachandrapuram (Table 7.8). So these villages show comparatively high sex ratios than in the year 1961.

Economic activity, which is dominant in the village, is another important aspect while comparing the male and female components of the population as well as the male and female workers.

Where the primary activities are dominant, the female workers are comparatively more in number especially as agricultural labour, whereas the secondary sector shows the dominance of male workers. Tertiary sector contains both male and female workers, even though the male workers are dominant the female workers are better in number than in the secondary sector (Table 7.11).

TABLE 7.7 : Average Household Size in Ramachandrapuram Zone, 1961-71

Village Name	*Year*	
	1961	*1971*
Pocharam	6.1	7.6
Muthangi	5.2	6.2
Patancheruvu	4.9	5.1
Patelguda	5.3	6.2
Ilapur	4.7	5.4
Bandalaguda	5.7	6.3
Kachireddipalle	7.3	6.3
Manmole	5.2	5.6
Ramachandrapuram (Rural)	5.8	5.5
BHEL Township	—	2.8
Aminpur	5.4	5.6
Chandanagar	5.6	4.7
Taranagar	5.7	4.2
Madeenaguda	5.3	4.8
Hafeezpet	8.7	5.4
Tellapur	6.1	6.2
Nalagandla	5.2	5.2
Serilingampalli	4.8	4.8
Kondapur	7.2	6.8
Gopanpalli	7.3	6.1
Kothaguda	6.5	5.6
Gachibowli	6.6	5.9
Mean	5.9	5.5

(*Source : Distt. Census Handbook*, Hyderabad & Medak 1961-71).

TABLE 7.8 : Distribution of Workers in Ramachandrapuram Zone, 1961-71

Village Name	*1961*			*1971*		
	Total	*Male*	*Female*	*Total*	*Male*	*Female*
Pocharam	427	217	210	497 (+16.39)	278 (+28.11)	219 (+4.29)
Muthangi	561	356	205	730 (+30.12)	443 (+24.48)	287 (+40.00)
Patancheruvu	1,470	1,016	454	1,788 (+21.63)	1,377 (+35.53)	411 (-43.00)
Patelguda	153	82	71	213 (+39.22)	119 (+45.12)	94 (+32.39)
Ilapur	123	73	50	114 (-7.32)	109 (+49.32)	5 (-90.00)
Bandalaguda	155	87	68	140 (-12.90)	120 (+37.93)	20 (-70.59)
Kachireddipalle	310	188	122	270 (-12.90)	210 (+11.70)	60 (-50.82)
Manmole	1,188	638	550	1,052 (-11.48)	760 (+19.12)	292 (-46.91)
Ramachandrapuram (Rural)	433	272	161	535 (+23.56)	439 (+61.40)	96 (-40.37)
BHEL Township	—	—	—	3,463 (—)	3,204 (—)	259 (—)
Aminpur	852	502	350	804 (-5.63)	628 (+25.10)	176 (-49.71)
Chandanagar	421	236	185	593 (+40.86)	383 (+62.29)	210 (+13.51)
Taranagar	192	127	65	389 (+102.60)	336 (+164.57)	53 (-18.46)
Madeenaguda	118	68	50	106 (-10.17)	63 (-7.35)	43 (-14.00)
Hafeezpet	434	290	144	375 (-13.36)	277 (-4.48)	98 (-31.94)
Tellapur	947	435	312	913 (-3.59)	737 (+16.06)	176 (-43.59)
Nalagandla	300	217	183	373 (+24.33)	297 (+36.87)	76 (-58.47)
Serilingampalli	378	247	131	679 (+76.63)	572 (+131.58)	107 (-18.32)
Kondapur	322	199	123	175 (-45.95)	165 (-17.09)	10 (-91.87)
Gopanpalli	609	349	260	317 (-47.95)	302 (-13.47)	15 (-94.23)
Kothaguda	278	165	133	177 (-36.33)	163 (-1.21)	14 (-87.61)
Gachibowli	121	81	40	97 (-19.83)	82 (+1.23)	15 (-62.50)
Mean	9,892	6,045	3,847	13,800 (+39.51)	11,064 (+83.03)	2,736 (-28.88)

(*Source:* *Distt. Census Handbook*, Hyderabad & Medak, 1961-1971).
Note: Figures in brackets show the percentage of growth rate.

TABLE 7.9 : Participation Rate in Ramachandrapuram Zone, 1961

Village Name	*Total*	*Male*	*Female*
Pocharam	64.80	64.20	65.42
Muthangi	47.23	62.57	33.12
Patancheruvu	40.42	54.77	25.48
Patelguda	56.04	62.60	50.00
Ilapur	58.30	68.87	47.62
Bandalaguda	55.76	63.04	48.57
Kachireddipalle	49.68	59.68	39.48
Manmole	59.79	64.57	55.05
Ramachandrapuram (Rural)	47.01	56.78	36.43
Aminpur	56.54	65.11	47.55
Chandanagar	63.79	71.95	55.72
Taranagar	45.82	65.13	29.02
Madeenaguda	65.92	73.91	57.47
Hafeezpet	53.85	69.88	36.83
Tellapur	47.14	63.44	30.95
Nalagandla	41.10	62.36	47.91
Serilingampalli	45.54	58.53	32.11
Kondapur	58.23	65.03	49.80
Gopanpalli	58.28	64.99	51.18
Kothaguda	59.15	69.33	48.71
Gachibowli	43.84	58.27	29.20
Mean	53.25	64.05	43.70

(*Source : Distt. Census Handbook*, Hyderabad & Medak, 1961).

TABLE 7.10 : Participation Rate in Ramachandrapuram Zone, 1971

Village Name	*Total*	*Male*	*Female*
Pocharam	62.52	64.15	59.03
Muthangi	49.53	61.27	38.22
Patancheruvu	35.38	53.35	17.11
Patelguda	55.04	59.80	50.00
Ilapur	29.77	55.33	2.69
Bandalaguda	31.18	52.63	9.05
Kachireddipalle	33.13	50.48	15.04
Manmole	39.13	56.80	22.02
Ramachandrapuram (Rural)	32.50	52.45	11.87
BHEL Township	31.07	55.40	4.83
Aminpur	41.08	62.80	18.39
Chandanagar	49.13	62.68	35.23
Taranagar	34.58	55.66	9.96

(*Contd.*)

(Contd.)

Madeenaguda	56.08	33.33	22.75
Hafeezpet	41.18	30.34	10.73
Tellapur	34.54	57.00	13.60
Nalagandla	34.03	55.04	13.10
Serilingampalli	39.59	60.92	13.79
Kondapur	31.08	29.31	1.78
Gopanpalli	30.81	29.35	1.46
Kothaguda	31.83	29.32	2.52
Gachibowli	28.20	23.84	4.36
Mean	38.70	49.60	17.16

(*Source : Distt. Census Handbook* Hyderabad & Medak, 1971).

TABLE 7.11 : Percentage Share of Total Workers in Ramachandrapuram Zone

Village Name	*1961*		*1971*	
	Male	*Female*	*Male*	*Female*
Pocharam	50.81	49.19	54.73	45.27
Muthangi	63.46	36.54	60.68	39.32
Patancheruvu	69.12	30.88	77.01	22.99
Patelguda	53.59	46.41	55.81	44.13
Ilapur	59.35	40.65	95.61	4.39
Bandalaguda	56.13	43.87	85.71	14.29
Kachireddipalle	60.65	39.35	77.78	22.22
Manmole	53.70	46.30	72.24	27.76
Ramachandrapuram (Rural)	62.82	37.18	82.06	17.94
BHEL Township	—	—	92.52	7.48
Aminpur	58.92	41.08	78.11	21.89
Chandanagar	56.06	43.94	64.59	35.41
Taranagar	66.15	33.95	86.38	13.62
Madeenaguda	57.13	42.37	59.43	40.57
Hafeezpet	66.82	33.18	73.67	26.33
Tellapur	67.05	32.95	80.72	19.28
Nalagandla	72.34	27.66	79.62	20.38
Serilingampalli	65.34	34.66	84.24	16.76
Kondapur	61.80	38.20	94.29	5.71
Gopanpalli	57.31	42.69	95.27	4.73
Kothaguda	59.35	40.65	92.09	7.91
Gachibowli	66.94	33.06	84.54	15.46
Mean	61.18	38.80	78.50	21.54

(*Source : Distt. Census Handbook* Hyderabad & Medak, 1961).

Population and Workers Correlation

Graph 7.1 shows the close relationship between the number of workers and the total population in each village. Wherever the number of workers are high, the population is also high. So it leads to a conclusion that the size of the population is depending on the size of the workers in the village in the present situation. The higher the number of workers the higher the population size, the lower the number of workers the lower the population size. This can be clearly observed in the Graph 7.1.

The highest population and number of workers were in Patancheruvu in 1961. Patancheruvu being a block headquarters in Medak district was a dominant settlement in the zone till 1961, but with the introduction of BHEL factory, the BHEL township became the highly populated settlement with highest number of workers engaged in the secondary sector activity of manufacturing. Patancheruvu has come down to the second place as far as total population and total number of workers are concerned. Next to these two major settlements comes Tellapur and Serilingampalli villages. The increase in the population of Tellapur village is understandable because its population even in 1961 was comparatively significant, but the increase in the population of Serilingampalli is mainly due to the establishment of few ancillary industries. The industrial activity increased the number of workers which increased the size of population.

Graph 7.1 relating the density of workers and the density of houses clearly indicates that higher the density of workers higher the density of houses. It clearly expresses that the work-home relationship is close in the zone and the workers try to live near their work-centres. This was true in the year 1961 as well as in the year 1971.

Take the case of Taranagar in the year 1971 when the settlement's density of workers as well as the density of houses were comparatively high, and the dominant economic activity was Trade and Commerce; which requires the nearness to the work-centre. So the predominant services are commercial like petty shops and miscellaneous stalls which can be easily combined for work and home needs. This is true in the case of other settlements also, but the degree of relationship varies with the type of dominant economic activity performed.

This work-home relationship and concentration of workers and houses became striking in the year 1971 than in the year 1961. This is mainly due to the major changes that occurred in the type of economic

GRAPH 7.1 : Demographic Characteristics of the Ramachandrapuram Zone 1

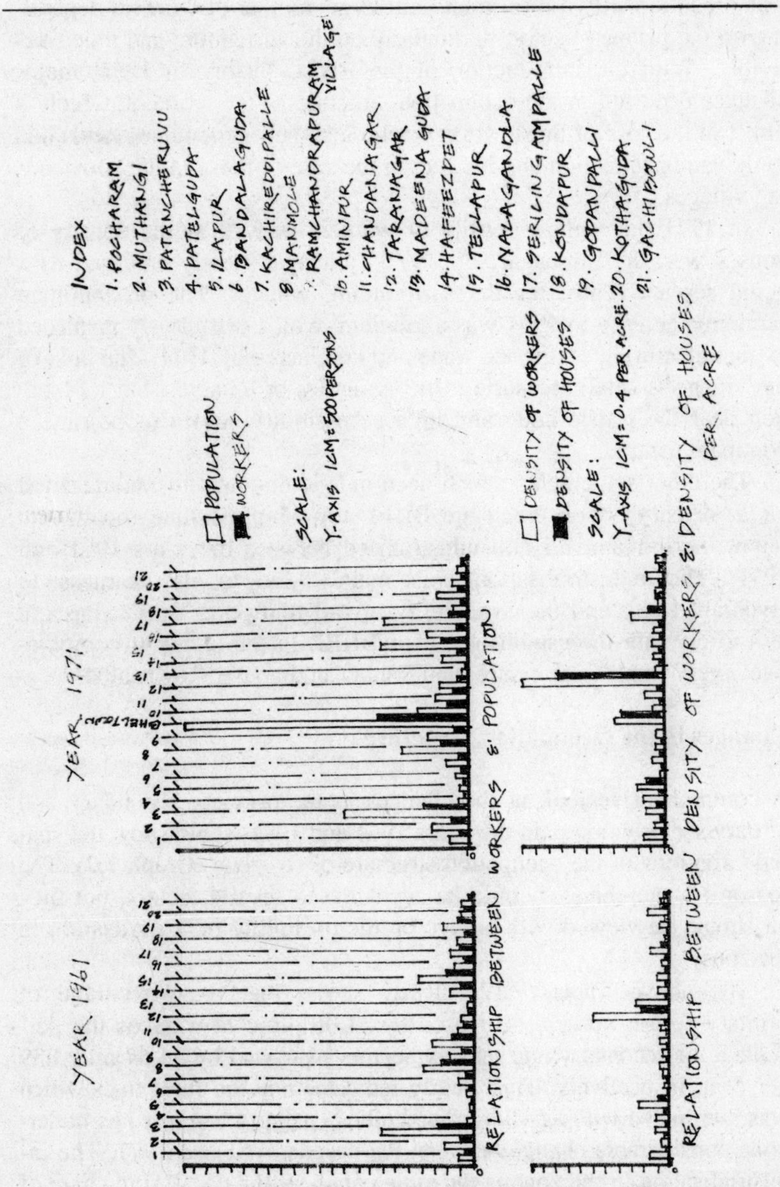

activities performed in the villages. Till the year 1961, the whole zone was predominantly a rural tract with large number of workers depending on the primary sector, particularly on the agriculture and allied activities. With the introduction of the BHEL factory in 1964, major changes occurred in the occupation structure of the workers, which is direct in the case of those workers who lost their agricultural lands due to the land acquisition and indirect in the case of those in the surrounding villages.

In 1971 the highest density of workers as well as the density of houses were in Taranagar. By 1971 Taranagar clearly emerged as a nodal service centre for the surrounding villages. The predominant economic activity in 1961 was agriculture which was clearly displaced by manufacturing sector and trade and commerce by 1971. The area of the village is small measuring 0.13 sq. miles or 83 acres, but its location near the traffic node and high accessibility helped to become a dominant centre.

The other settlements which need mentioning next to Taranagar as far as density is concerned are BHEL township, Serilingampalli and Ilapur. Serilingampalli got industrialised between the years 1961 and 1971. The industrialisation was mainly due to its nearness to Hyderabad city and the availability of rail transport. Thus it has got less to do with the establishment of BHEL factory. This is comparatively very small work centre than Ramachandrapuram township.

Changes in the Occupation Structure

A comprehensive look at the changes in the primary, secondary and tertiary sector workers in the years 1961 and 1971 would show the spatial variations in the occupation structure of the zone (Graph 7.2). The reason for the changes could be attributed to several factors, but they all should be viewed with an eye on the prevailing industrialisation in the zone.

The above Table (7.12) clearly shows that the percentage of primary sector workers decreased by 31.06 per cent whereas the percentage of secondary and tertiary sectors increased by 26.67 and 4.39 per cent, respectively. This clearly indicates that the rural tract which was dominated with agriculture and allied category workers has undergone considerable change between the decade 1961 and 1971. The industrialisation in the zone is the main cause for the decreasing share of primary activities. The location of the basic industry had considerable impact on the prevailing agricultural activities. It directly snatched away the agricultural land-holdings for its existence and indirectly created an impetus for industrial growth in the surrounding villages.

TABLE 7.12 : Comparative View of the Industrial Sectors, 1961-71*

	Primary	*Secondary*	*Tertiary*
1961	77.13	11.06	11.81
1971	46.07	37.73	16.20
Percentage Variation	-31.06	+26.67	+4.39

(*Source*: District Census Handbook - Medak & Hyderabad 1961-71).
* figure are mentioned in percentages to the total workers.

Graphs 7.2 showing the percentage of workers engaged in primary, secondary and tertiary activities could be examined to understand the changes in each village between the decade 1961 and 1971.

As observed earlier and also from the graph, the number of workers in the primary activities decreased in the zone except in few villages like Pocharam, Madeenaguda, Bandalaguda and Gopanpalli. The increase in these few villages could be the push of unemployed agricultural labour from the villages; which started taking the secondary sector activities in preference to the primary sector activities.

The villages which have shown steep decline in the number of workers of the primary sector are Ramachandrapuram, Taranagar and Serilingampalli. The decline in Ramachandrapuram is due to the establishment of BHEL factory. Taranagar and Serilingampalli started specialising in trade and commerce and manufacturing, respectively, by 1971. Thus, the steep decline in the primary sector workers is also an indication of the settlements inclination to specialise in some other activity than the primary sector.

There is an overall increase in the number of workers in the secondary sector between 1961 and 1971. The highest number is found obviously in Ramachandrapuram followed by Serilingampalli and Taranagar. There is a considerable reduction of secondary sector workers in Madeenaguda between 1961 and 1971 because the village got more number in the primary sector by 1971. Similarly in the case of Gopanpalli, Bandalaguda and Pocharam villages; which are dominated by primary sector workers. Thus there is a contrast between the primary and secondary sectors, a fall in one sector resulted in the increase of another sector.

GRAPH 7.2 : Demographic Characteristics of the Ramachandrapuram Zone 2

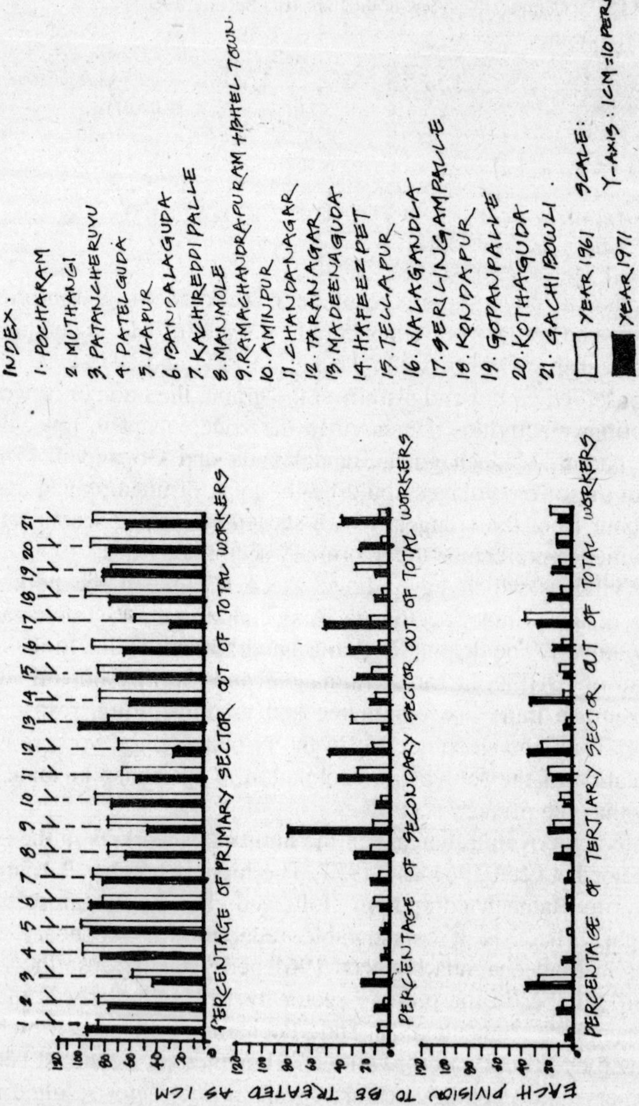

From these two graphs showing the changes of primary and secondary sectors between 1961-71, the following conclusions could be made :

(a) Primary sector workers are dominant in Pocharam and Bandalaguda in 1971.
(b) Secondary sector workers are more in number in Ramachandrapuram, Taranagar and Serilingampalli.

GRAPH 7.3 : Decadal changes in the Nine Industrial Categories of Ramachandrapuram Zone

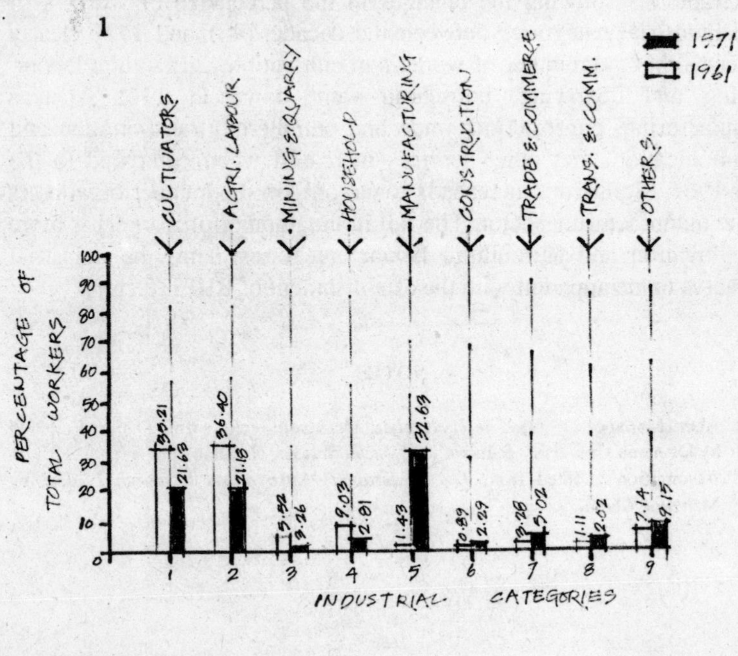

The number of workers in the tertiary sector were dominant in Patancheruvu, Serilingampalli and Taranagar in 1961, but in 1971 the number of workers in the services went down comparatively in Serilingampalli with the emergence of Taranagar as service centre. In 1971 Patancheruvu, Taranagar and Hafeezpet emerged as important centres for service population. The service population is more in Patancheruvu mainly because of its status as a block headquarters in Medak district. So there is a steady increase in the number of workers in services between the decade 1961-71.

The percentage of increase of service population is very low when compared to the secondary sector. The decadal percentage of increase for the tertiary sector is just 4.39 whereas for the secondary sector it is 26.67. This shows the inadequate development of the tertiary sector in the zone. One encouraging trend is the emergence of Taranagar as a service centre. The main asset of this village is its position at a node where the new Bombay and old Bombay highways from Hyderabad meet, which gives the settlement the advantage of easy accessibility.

Graph 7.3 showing the changes in the percentage of workers of nine industrial categories between the decade 1961 and 1971 clearly indicates that the number of workers in cultivation, agricultural labour, mining and quarrying, household went down in 1971 whereas manufacturing, construction, trade and commerce, transportation and communication, and other services increased when compared to the year 1961. Significant increase is found only in the number of workers in the manufacturing sector. The fall in the number of workers is more in cultivation and agricultural labour categories. Thus the industrial impact is made apparent with the establishment of BHEL factory.

NOTES

1. Alam Manzoor (1969). *The Hyderabad Metropolitan Research Project* Prepared by Osmania University & Institute of Asian Studies, Hyderabad.
2. Assumption adopted from *The Hyderabad Metropolitan Research Project* by Manzoor Alam.

8

CENTRALITY AND FUNCTIONAL CLASSIFICATION OF VILLAGE

"THE PROPORTION of labour force of a city engaged in performing a service is perhaps the best means of measuring the distribution of that activity by using the following :[1]

Si = 100 e/W
e = Population engaged in an activity in a town.
W = Total working population of the town.
(in the present case village is substituted in place of town)."

An index value above the mean indicates the specialisation whose intensity could be measured by the standard deviation. If the standard deviation is more the activity is highly concentrated and if the standard deviation is less then it shows no specialisation or uniformity in the economic activity performed over the space. However, the intensity of the deviation shows the real picture of specialisation or non-specialisation.

The same method is adopted in the case of Ramachandrapuram one by finding out the functional index for each village. The functional index for all the 21 villages and the BHEL township has been calculated for the years 1961 and 1971. The nine industrial categories of the census has been divided into eight categories by including cultivators, agricultural and livestock under the category of agriculture and allied activities. Tables 8.1 and 8.2 show the means and standards deviations for the years 1961 and 1971.

The highest mean value goes to Agriculture and allied activities followed by household, mining and quarrying, other services, trade and commerce, transportation and communication, manufacturing and construction. The highest standard deviation goes to agriculture, fol

TABLE 8.1 : Means and Standards Deviation for the Year 1961

	Agri-culture	*Mining & Quarry*	*House-hold*	*Manu-factur-ing*	*Const-ruction*	*Trade & Comm-erce*	*Trans-porta-tion & Commu-nica-tion*	*Other Services*
Mean	71.82	6.27	8.42	1.12	0.87	2.93	1.29	5.25
Standard Deviation	15.73	7.61	6.84	1.18	2.8	2.66	2.35	5.16
Mean + 1 SD	87.65	13.88	15.26	2.30	3.67	5.69	3.64	10.41
Mean + 2 SD	103.88	21.49	22.10	3.48	6.47	8.35	5.99	15.57
Mean + 3 SD		29.10	28.94		9.27		8.34	20.73
& Above		36.71					10.69	25.99

lowed by mining and quarrying, household, other services, construction, trade and commerce, transportation and communication and manufacturing. This clearly shows the insignificance of the manufacturing sector till 1961. The high standard deviation in agriculture cannot be said as a tendency for specialisation because the intensity of deviation goes up only to mean + 2 SD. This is explained in detail later.

TABLE 8.2 : Means and Standards Deviations for the Year 1971

	Agri-culture	*Mining & Quar-rying*	*House-hold*	*Manu-factur-ing*	*Const-ruction*	*Trade & Comm-erce*	*Trans-porta-tion & Commu-nica-tion*	*Other Services*
Mean	61.84	3.13	3.22	16.08	2.56	4.95	1.81	6.65
Standard Deviation	24.16	4.35	2.43	18.18	4.05	4.57	2.37	5.93
Mean + 1 SD	86.0	7.48	5.65	34.26	6.61	9.52	4.18	12.58
Mean + 2 SD	110.16	11.83	8.08	52.44	10.66	14.09	6.55	18.51
Mean + 3 SD		16.18	10.51	70.62	14.71	18.66	8.92	24.44
& Above				88.80		23.23	11.29	

The highest mean once again goes to agriculture and allied activities followed by manufacturing, services, trade and commerce, household, mining and quarrying, construction and transportation and communication. The standard deviation is highest for agriculture, followed by manufacturing, services, trade and commerce, mining and quarrying, construction, household and transportation and communication. The impact of industrialisation is obvious with comparatively high standard deviation than in the year 1961 in agriculture, manufacturing, services and trade and commerce. One significant feature by the year 1971 in Ramachandrapuram zone is the specialisation of manufacturing activity and simultaneous tendency for specialisation in trade and commerce and services, which indicate the urban characteristics of the area.

Graphs 8.1 and 8.2 show clearly the comparative picture of eight industrial categories in each village in the years 1961 and 1971. The changes under each category in the zone is clearly explained in the following paragraphs for the years 1961 and 1971.

Agriculture and Mining and Quarrying

Agriculture – Year 1961

The mean value is 71.82 and the deviation from the mean is up to Mean + 2 SD. Though there is some deviation, it was not significant indicating the absence of any kind of specialisation.

– Year 1971

The mean value is 61.84 and the standard deviation is 24.16 indicating comparatively a high degree of standard deviation than in 1961. The deviation is only up to Mean + 2 SD showing that the intensity of specialisation of the economic activity is less and there are certain concentrated pockets, like, Pocharam, Bandalaguda and Madeenaguda. This concentration may be due to the forced migration of agricultural labourers from their previous villages with the introduction of industrial activity in the zone.

Mining and Quarrying – Year 1961

The mean value is 6.27 and the standard deviation is 7.61. So the

GRAPH 8.1 : Functional Classification of the Villages 1

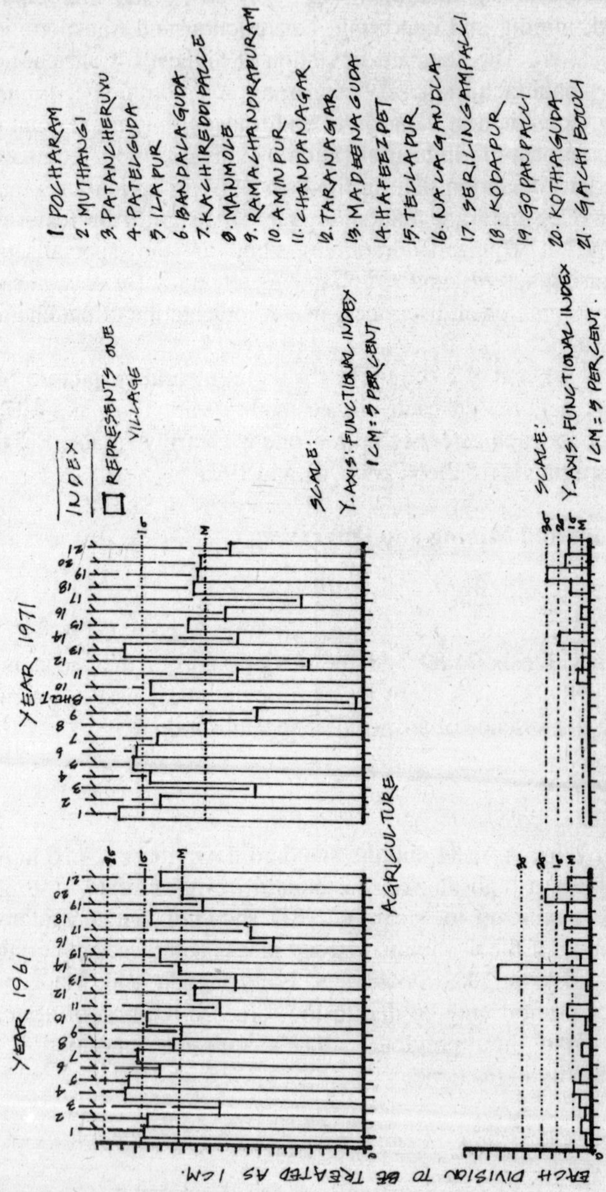

GRAPH 8.2 : Functional Classification of the Villages 2

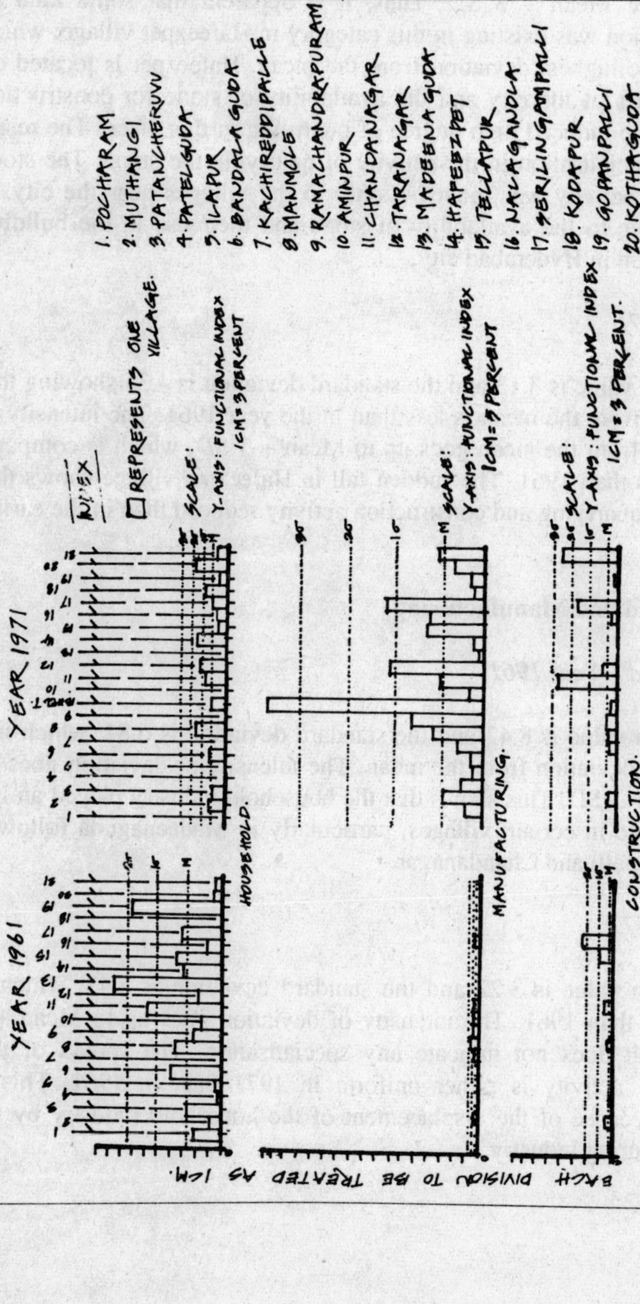

deviation from the mean is considerable and the intensity of deviation goes above Mean + 3 SD. Thus, it is apparent that some kind of specialisation was existing in this category in Hafeezpet village; which has got the highest deviation from the mean. Hafeezpet is located on the outskirts of the city and the availability of stone for construction should have induced high degree of quarrying in this place. The result was its specialisation in the activity of quarrying the stone. The stone quarrying activity was intensive only in the villages near the city. It may be due to the availability of stone and their use in the building construction in Hyderabad city.

– Year 1971

The mean value is 3.13 and the standard deviation is 4.35 showing that deviation from the mean is less than in the year 1961. The intensity of deviation from the mean goes up to Mean + 3 SD, which is comparatively less than 1961. The sudden fall in Hafeezpet village shows that the stone quarrying and construction activity reduced than in the earlier years.

Household and Manufacturing

Household – Year 1961

The mean value is 8.42 and the standard deviation is 6.84; which is a moderate deviation from the mean. The intensity of deviation goes up to Mean + 3 SD. This shows that the household industry played an important role in certain villages, particularly in Madeenaguda followed by Gopanpalli and Chandanagar.

– Year 1971

The mean value is 3.22 and the standard deviation is 2.43; which is very less than 1961. The intensity of deviation goes up to Mean + 3 SD, but it does not indicate any specialisation. The spread of this economic activity is rather uniform in 1971 than in 1961. This is mainly because of the displacement of the household industry by the manufacturing industry.

Manufacturing – Year 1961

The mean value is 1.12 and the standard deviation is 1.18, which is very less. The intensity of deviation goes up to Mean + 2 SD, clearly indicating that the manufacturing industry played an insignificant role and the household industry had a lead till 1961. Though the spread of the activity was not uniform, the less standard deviation shows that it was almost even wherever it was existing. There were six villages in 1961 which did not possess a single worker in this category, but by 1971 these villages also had enough number of workers engaged in the manufacturing category.

– Year 1971

The mean value is 16.08 and the standard deviation is 18.3; which is comparatively very high than in 1961. The specialisation intensity goes beyond Mean + 3 SD and Graph 8.2 clearly shows the specialisation of this activity in BHEL township. With the establishment of BHEL factory, it pulled up the workers in the manufacturing sector in the surrounding villages also. Thus these villages also show good number of workers engaged in this economic activity. Next to BHEL township stands Serilingampalli and Taranagar as far as the percentage of workers in manufacturing sector is concerned.

Construction and Trade & Commerce

Construction – Year 1961

The mean value is 0.87 and the standard deviation is 2.8; which is a moderate deviation. The intensity of deviation goes up to Mean + 3 SD, showing that there was some intensity of the activity at Serilingampalli village. This may be due to the establishment of few industries and construction of houses around the year 1961.

– Year 1971

The mean value is 2.56 and the standard deviation is 4.05; which is comparatively high than in 1961. The intensity of specialisation of the activity goes up to Mean + 3 SD. Thus the specialisation intensity is almost the same as 1961, but the activity is concentrated at few places.

Chandanagar stand first followed by Gachibowli and Serilingampalli. The intensity of the activity in Chandanagar may be due to the establishment of BHEL factory at Ramachandrapuram. Many workers could not get housing accommodation in the township, so they started purchasing plots for constructing houses in Chandanagar which is adjacent to the BHEL township.

Trade and Commerce

– Year 1961

The mean value is 2.93 and the standard deviation is 2.66, which is not considerable. The intensity of deviation goes up to Mean + 2 SD, showing no specialisation in the activity. Thus it is clear that there was no core centre to serve the needs of the surrounding villages, every village had its own trade and commerce activity limited to meet its needs.

– Year 1971

The mean is 4.95 and the standard deviation is 4.57 which is comparatively higher than the year 1961. The intensity of specialisation goes above Mean + 3 SD, clearly showing specialisation of trade and commerce activity in Taranagar; which became a nodal service centre of trade and commerce for the surrounding villages. It is followed by Ramachandrapuram and Patancheruvu. So it is clear that trade and commerce activity made a significant progress during the decade 1961-71.

Transportation and Communication and Services

Transportation & Communication – Year 1961

The mean value is 1.29 and the standard deviation is 2.85; which is considerable when compared with the spread of the activity. The intensity of deviation goes above Mean + 3 SD, showing the concentration of the activity in Serilingampalli. It is followed by Kothaguda and Taranagar. The high accessibility of road transportation and the location of railway station could be the reasons for its intensity and concentration.

– Year 1971

The mean value is 1.81 and the standard deviation is 2.37; which is almost same as the earlier year 1961. The standard deviation goes above Mean + 3 SD. Serilingampalli still continues to be the dominant centre for this activity whereas the other two villages Taranagar and Kothaguda reduced their share considerably. The specialisation of Taranagar in Trade and Commerce could be an important reason for its fall in the share of this activity. Patancheruvu being a block headquarters raised its share of workers in this economic activity by 1971.

Services – Year 1961

The mean value is 5.25 and the standard deviation is 5.16. The intensity of deviation goes above Mean + 3 SD. Patancheruvu as a block headquarters has got the highest number of workers in this category engaged in the services like administration, etc. This village was followed by Taranagar and Serilingampalli, where there could be more number of workers engaged under miscellaneous services because they did not specialise till 1971 in any activity.

– Year 1971

The mean value is 6.65 and the standard deviation is 5.93; which is almost same as the earlier year 1961. The deviation from the mean goes up to Mean + 3 SD. Patancheruvu leads above all other villages in 1971 also, but the specialisation intensity was reduced comparatively than in the year 1961. Hafeezpet stands second in this economic activity. The lower specialisation intensity shows that the service sector did not grow to the required level when compared to the manufacturing sector.

Functional Centrality of the Settlements

An activity becomes significant for a village not merely in comparison to other activities of the same village but also with reference to all the villages of an area to which the village belongs. Hence to determine the quantitative functional significance of a village in a region, regional functional share of each centre in the form of percentage has been calculated and the functional centrality is found as follows :[2]

GRAPH 8.3 : Functional Classification of the Villages 3

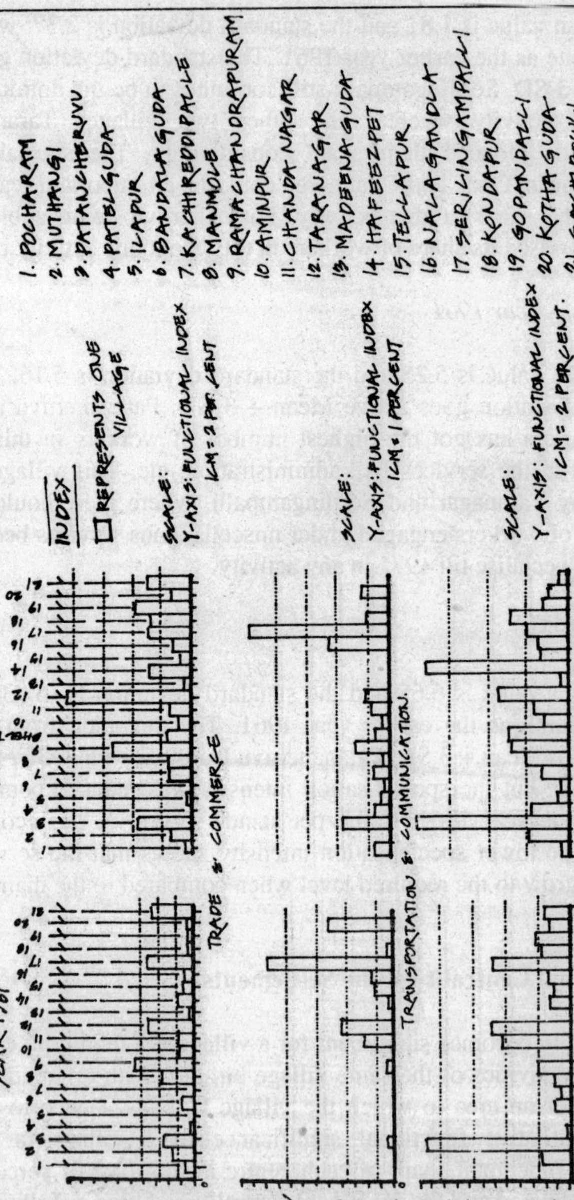

$Ci = rSi$
r = regional ratio index = $100\ e/\Sigma$
e = population of a village engaged in a function
Σe = total population of the region engaged in that function, and
Si = functional specialisation

To determine the regional position, *Ci* mean and therefrom standard deviation up to three degrees have been calculated and arranged in five descending orders in their respective activities.

1st order	3 SD and above
2nd order	2 SD and above
3rd order	1 SD and above
4th order	above the mean
5th order	mean and below.

The functional centrality for three important categories, in manufacturing, trade and commerce and services, is found for the year 1971.

The details are shown in Table 8.3

TABLE 8.3 : Functional Centrality of the Villages, Year 1971

	Manufacturing	*Trade & Commerce*	*Services*	*Order*
Mean	282.79	36.11	64.58	5
Standard Deviation	24.79	19.51	55.46	4
Mean + 1 SD	307.58	55.62	120.04	3
Mean + 2 SD	332.37	75.13	175.50	2
Mean + 3 SD	357.16	94.60	230.96	1

Observations

Manufacturing

1st order - BHEL township

Rest of the villages are below the mean showing the dominance of the factory on the surrounding industrial activity.

Trade and Commerce

Ist order - None.
2nd order - Taranagar, Patancheruvu & Ramachandrapuram.

Taranagar has got an edge over the other two, which can be found in the (Table 8.4) shown later.

3rd order - BHEL town
4th order - Serilingampalli.

Services

1st order - Patancheruvu
2nd order - BHEL
3rd order - Hafeezpet

Rest are below the mean.

The functional centrality of each village is as shown in Table 8.4.

TABLE 8.4 : Functional Centrality of the Villages in Ramachandrapuram Zone 1971

Village	*Manufacturing*	*Trade & Commerce*	*Services*
Pocharam	0.02	1.05	0.78
Muthangi	5.60	12.35	23.96
Patancheruvu	90.45	196.29	833.92
Patelguda	2.70	-	6.28
Ilapur	0.32	0.02	0.28
Bandalaguda	0.39	-	0.23
Kachireddipalli	5.19	0.39	2.06
Mamole	85.23	18.80	35.82
Ramachandrapuram (Rural)	89.50	113.97	32.70
BHEL township	5434.50	68.34	216.83
Aminpur	4.48	4.60	10.07
Chanda Nagar	35.17	10.73	14.51
Taranagar	107.10	225.76	37.57
Madeenaguda	0.02	0.02	0.08
Hafeezpet	1.00	25.99	145.39
Tellapur	98.21	4.04	13.19

Village	*Manufacturing*	*Trade & Commerce*	*Services*
Nalagandla	38.99	4.67	5.44
Serilingampalli	209.74	46.99	24.68
Kondapur	0.45	11.86	11.61
Gopanpalli	1.56	38.25	3.60
Kothaguda	4.07	2.95	1.63
Gachibowli	6.66	7.29	0.08
Mean	282.79	39.72	64.58

NOTES

1. The method is adopted from Pyare Ram (1980). 'Functional Classification of Towns of Bundelkhand'/*National Geographer*, 15, June. Allahabad University.
2. *Ibid.*

9

PLANNING APPROACH TO RAMACHANDRAPURAM-PATANCHERUVU ZONE

THERE IS a need to clarify certain important aspects whenever a new area has been planned for development. There are many new town concepts and each has got its own importance and purpose to serve. The evaluations of several new towns have been discussed in the earlier chapter. Now, before adopting any indicative development policies, there is a need to suggest a planning framework on which this particular area is going to be developed. By now, new town development has become a most controversial issue and its significance is repeatedly put to question. To clear these doubts is important before indulging in any development at Ramachandrapuram.

Cities were planned in the past and are being planned at present. Cities in the past did not increase as fast as they do today. The transportation technology has expanded the city's growth. With the fast expansion of the cities, the organisation of functions and services becomes increasingly difficult. The increasing density and activities force the urban expansion eating away the rural hinterland and, thus, there is a continuous urban invasion over the agricultural land. New additions to the cities either in the shape of towns or extensions have become a must to receive the growing population and activities.

Industries are usually not allowed to come up within the municipal limits with few exceptions. So initially they started spreading on the peripheral areas of the municipal limits. With the availability of good transportation and other development incentives, they started going further away. The commuting distances started increasing. It became a tough exercise for the workers to commute long distances regularly, so they started settling down near the work centres. The public transportation system could not really cope up with the increasing traffic. Railways are the only efficient rapid-transit system available to regular commuters in India, and this has been limited to few big metropolitan cities, like, Bombay, Calcutta and Madras. This system is yet to develop to the required extent in other metropolitan cities.

Organising the workers around the work centres has become a necessity to avoid heavy commutation and increasing transportation problems. This means providing mass housing, infrastructure and social service facilities. The development cost of the same is enormous for a single government authority to bear. In addition to this large-scale acquisition of land will take away the livelihood of those who depend on agricultural land.

This is the case in Ramachandrapuram. The establishment of BHEL factory, the growth of ancillary industries and the policy to develop Patancheruvu as industrial area have led to heavy concentration of industrial workers. Many workers commute regularly from Hyderabad and some reside in the surrounding villages. There is a certain limit beyond which heavy commutation should be avoided otherwise it may lead to transportation problems and breakdown of services as it happened in the case of Bombay. These are the circumstances which compel the development of the area. Even if the government is hesitant to take action, the private developers are on toes to grab the chance leading to irrational growth. So the need to regulate the development in this area is very essential leaving aside the questions, like, whether it will be a satellite town or ring town. It does not matter whether it can be called a satellite or ring town as long as it serves the above purpose.

Once it is accepted that organising the development in this area is essential, then the development of this area should be in relation to Hyderabad because it falls under the metropolitan influence.

The following aspects have been taken into consideration before suggesting the development policies in the area. The whole development should take place keeping in view the following five aspects :

1. Function
2. Commercial core
3. Growth axis
4. Self-containment
5. Regional employment centre

1. *Function*

Function is an important base on which the area develops.

Mr. Mitra has classified all the towns of 1961 into the following four categories :

(A) Manufacturing town,
(B) Trade and Transportation town,
(C) Service town,
(D) Agriculture town.

The criterion he adopted for the classification of the towns is as shown in the Table 9.1. To calculate the percentages in the present case Ramachandrapuram zone has been taken into consideration. It is found that the percentage of workers in IV, V(a)(b), VI together exceeds the percentage of workers under B or C by more than 20 per cent. The details are as mentioned below :

			No. of workers
IV	Mining and Quarrying	...	210
V	(a) Household industry	...	388
	(b) Manufacturing	...	4,503
VI	Construction	...	316
			5,417
VII	Trade & Commerce	...	693
VIII	Transportation & Communication	...	279
			972
IX	Other services	...	1,263

(figures are as per 1971 Census)

2. *Commercial Core*

Every organic growth has got a core from where it spreads. The urban core develops in the transportation node and spreads all along the transportation routes deviating from it. This is true in the case of

TABLE 9.1 : Mitrai Classified of Towns 1961

Category	*Group of towns*	*Census industrial category of workers*	*Criterion on for group*
1	2	3	4
A	Manufacturing	III Mining, Quarrying, Livestocks & forestry IV Household industry V Manufacturing other than household VI Construction	The percentage of workers in the four Census industrial categories, specified in Col.3, exceeds the percentage of workers under B or C by 20 per cent or more.
B	Trade & Transportation	VII Trade & Commerce VIII Transportation, Storage & Commerce	The percentage of workers in two Census industrial categories, specified in Col.3, together exceeds the percentage of workers under A or C by 20 per cent or more.
C	Service	IX Other services	The percentage of workers in Census industrial categories, specified in Col.3, exceeds the percentage of workers under A or B by 20 per cent or more.
D	Agriculture	I Cultivator II Agricultural labourers	The towns whose proportion of workers in categories, specified in Col.3, remains higher than that of workers in any other three groups A, B and C.

(*Source* : Bose Ashish *India's Urbanisation 1901-2001*, Tata McGraw-Hill Publishing Co., Ltd., New Delhi.)

Ramachandrapuram also. Developing core is a real advantage but moulding it to meet the future needs of the area is more important and it should be viewed once again in the context of CBD of Hyderabad city.

W. Burns outlined a four-tier system of intra-urban shopping centres. They were :[1]

1. Town Centre (the equivalent of CBD)
2. District Centre
3. Neighbourhood Centre
4. Sub-centre

The regional influence of Hyderabad CBD is so large that it embraces Ramachandrapuram. So the commercial core at Ramachandrapuram cannot be a parallel CBD of Hyderabad city. The core of Ramachandrapuram could be a district centre next in the order after CBD in the hierarchy of shopping centres mention above.

Another neighbourhood centre should be developed at Patancheruvu because it is the important settlement next to Ramachandrapuram in the zone as far as the population and function are concerned (Map 9.1).

3. *Growth Axis*

The growth and the direction of growth is very important for planning. In the case of Ramachandrapuram the growth is in three directions from the commercial core of Taranagar. The dynamic growth axis is on both sides of the Hyderabad-Bombay highway between Ramachandrapuram and Patancheruvu. Many industries are located on this axis and the commercial services are coming up fast on both sides of the road. To regulate the growth of industries and shops along this axis is important.

The next axis of growth is along the highway on the eastern side passing through Chandanagar village. Here the construction of individual houses and housing colonies on both sides of the road is dominant. The land value is particularly very high around the commercial core of Taranagar. There is lot of unauthorised construction in Chandnagar village because of its nearness to the BHEL factory. There is a need to regulate the housing development along this axis.

MAP 9.1 : Growth Pattern of Ramachandrapuram-Patancheruvu Area

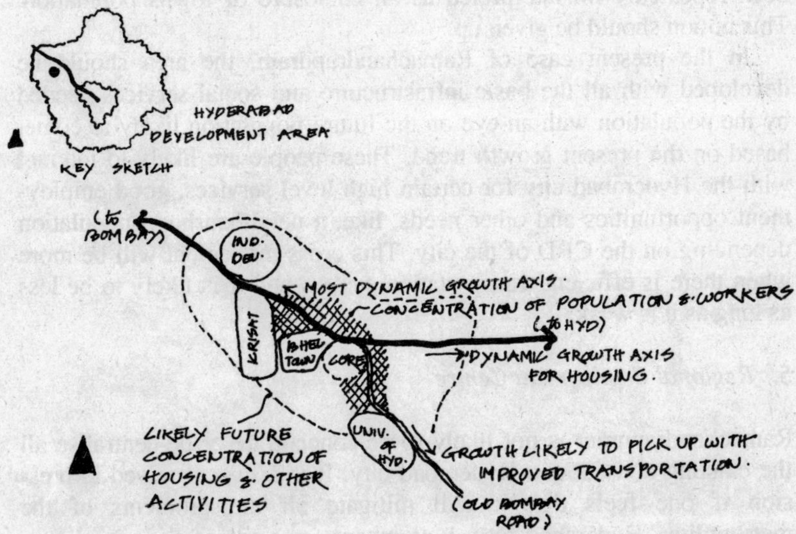

Sketch Showing the Growth Pattern of Ramachandrapuram — Patancheruvu Area

The other axis of growth is along the old Bombay-Hyderabad road, which is not as dynamic as the other two. This may be mainly due to the lack of transportation frequency. The other two axes have got good road and frequency of transportation when compared to this axis. However, most of the area in the zone along the road is occupied by University of Hyderabad and the completion of their University campus may stimulate growth on the other side of the road. At present the growth pattern is not very clear along this axis.

4. *Self-containment*

Self-containment of a settlement has been often misconceived as closing of outside employment opportunities and services to the local population. None of our towns and cities, whether Bombay, Delhi or Madras, is self-contained in that sense of the word. Interaction among the settlements is important and cross movement of people is always essential for higher economic development. It has been a practice among the planners to say, whenever a new town is planned, that it will be self-contained. Though their expression may be correct but it has been repeatedly misinterpreted as an enclosure of towns population. This notion should be given up.

In the present case of Ramachandrapuram, the area should be developed with all the basic infrastructure and social services needed by the population with an eye on the future population likely to come, based on the present growth trend. These people are likely to interact with the Hyderabad city for certain high level services, good employment opportunities and other needs, like, a neighbourhood population depending on the CBD of the city. This cross-movement will be more when there is efficient transportation system and it is likely to be less as long as it is weak.

5. *Regional Employment Centre*

Ramachandrapuram is not likely to de-concentrate or de-centralise all the existing activities in Hyderabad city. It is a misconceived impression if one feels that it will mitigate all the problems of the metropolitan Hyderabad city. It is meant for none of these two purposes but to organise the future growth of Hyderabad city.

Organising the urban growth is essential and the city cannot grow extremely mono-centric. There is every need to develop smaller centres in spite of the dominance of the core. These small centres can cater to the needs of some population, which need not depend on the main city to meet all its needs. Ramachandrapuram can receive that future population which would have otherwise gone into the city increasing its problems. Ramachandrapuram is likely to serve the following purposes :

(a) Self-contained for essential services,
(b) as a good employment centre of some regional importance,
(c) as a good location for the industries which would like to utilise the scale economics of the Hyderabad city.

Ramachandrapuram is undoubtedly under the influence of Hyderabad city but it has got an influence region of its own from where the people are likely to move to the town for employment affecting the economy of the villages. Every important investment in Ramachandrapuram should take care of this fact.

The boundaries of villages, *taluks* and districts are made for administrative convenience, but the economic investment impacts are likely to cross and overlap these boundaries. Under such circumstances the concerned administrative authorities should strongly protect the welfare of their respective populations.

NOTE

1. Carter Harold, (1976). *The Study of Urban Geography*, Edward Arnold Rtd., London.

10

INDICATIVE DEVELOPMENT POLICIES FOR RAMACHANDRAPURAM -PATANCHERUVU ZONE

THE DEVELOPMENT of Ramachandrapuram-Patancheruvu as a town should not be treated like a project town, and the active participation of the private sector is also necessary. The co-operation of all the three districts involved in the Hyderabad development area is important. The development should be included in the structure plan of Hyderabad development area. The development of Ramachandrapuram-Patancheruvu should be treated as a part of the Hyderabad development area and not in isolation.

Based on the study and analysis made in the earlier chapters, the following indicative development policies are suggested for Ramachandrapuram-Patancheruvu to develop as a unit. Each indicative development policy is marked on the map wherever necessary.

Acquisition of Agricultural Land

Whenever there is urban invasion, the agricultural landholders are the worst sufferers because land is the only source of livelihood for them. Nearly 33 per cent of the land in Ramachandrapuram zone is still under agriculture. So there is a need to protect the interests of the agricultural workers and the following measures should be taken up for the same :

(a) The following villages have got more than 85 per cent of workers depending on agriculture out of the total workers in the village :

It should be seen that least harm is done to these villages due to the non-agricultural urban activities and the agricultural land should be protected otherwise it may lead to the displacement of workers in agricultural activities.

Village	*Percentage of workers*	*Total workers*
* Patelguda	93.46	213
* Ilapur	92.69	114
* Aminpur	85.80	804
* Pocharam	86.81	497
* Muthangi	85.21	730

(b) Another important aspect is the conservation of wet land from non-agricultural uses. The following villages have got the highest percentage of wet land out of the total wet land in Ramachandrapuram zone :

Village		*Percentage*
* Aminpur	...	28.56
* Patancheruvu	...	19.04

The wet land in these areas should be avoided for non-agriculture uses. The same land could be used for productive urban uses like vegetables, fruits, etc.

(c) The village sites should be left as they are to avoid the dislocation of the villagers, so that unity and identity of each village could be retained. The non-agricultural land-uses should be properly integrated with the existing village sites.

(d) Ramachandrapuram-Patancheruvu zone has got 23 villages, out of which 12 villages are in the jurisdiction of Rangareddy district. In these villages Serinalagandla is uninhabited and Kanchigachibowli village is almost occupied by University of Hyderabad. The other 11 villages are in the jurisdiction of Medak district. Out of these 11 villages Kachireddipalle and Manmde villagers are completely evacuated for BHEL and ICRISAT.

These villagers are rehabilitated in the Ramachandrapuram new settlement under the administrative control of Ramachandrapuram *Panchayat.*

The respective district administrative authorities should take the responsibility of providing employment to those workers who are displaced from agricultural activities and deprived of their own agricultural land. The authorities should draft a policy to see that the industries which are located in the area could provide employment to these workers because most of them are illiterate and unskilled.

Development of Commercial Core at Taranagar

The identified centre for trade and commerce is Taranagar and it is situated at the traffic node. It is not developed to the required extent Though it does not fall under the first order as far as the centrality of trade and commerce is concerned, it has got an edge over Patancheruvu and Ramachandrapuram; which also belong to the second order in the centrality function of trade and commerce. The type of shops existing at present is an evidence for that. There are over 50 permanent shops at present and the variety of shops include general stores, textile, T.V., brandy, arrack, hotels, restaurants, medical, hardware, mechanic, flour mills, book stall,s printing press, chit fund, bank, optician, cinema theatre.

(a) The present commercial core at Taranagar should be upgraded to the level of district centre for shopping in view of the future population (Table 10.1).

The growth rate of population between 1961 and 1971 in the area was 97.81 and if the same growth rate continued then the population in 1981 of 75,372 would be 1,49,093 in 1991. Thus, the population will be around one-and-half lakhs by 1991 in the area.

Keeping this in view the core should be developed to meet the increasing needs with variety of shops. The required standards are mentioned below and they should be adopted with some flexibility. There should be some provision for hawkers and vendors around the core along with the market space.

The peculiar feature at present is the combination of house and shop, and while organising the shopping centre it should be seen that these people are not harmed. The road encroachment should be strictly prohibited.

(b) The commercial development is likely to take place all along the three highways deviating from Taranagar. A radius of one km. can be taken from the core to check the encroachment of commercial shops on the highway. The commercial development along the highway should strictly follow the minimum set back regulations so that irregular commercial growth could be avoided.

This area could be taken as an action area before developing organised shopping and market space for perishable goods.

(c) Developing a shopping centre at sector level at Patancheruvu is essential in view of its fast growth. The recent industrial development led to its fast growth and its population was around 8,000 in 1981 census. The industrial workers in this area will be provided housing by Andhra Pradesh Industrial Infrastructure Corporation with the assistance of HUDCO. In view of the industrial population to be housed and the future service population, there is a need to preplan the shopping facilities.

The importance of the settlement next to BHEL town as far as population and function are concerned, and also its own centrality in trade and commerce activity next to Taranagar emphasises the need to develop shopping facilities catering not only to the needs of the local population but also to the surrounding villages.

Future Industrial Development Policy

The Andhra Pradesh Government policy is to develop the industries in the Medak district for economic development and APIIC recognised Patancheruvu as a potential industrial nucleus.

The future industrial development is likely to take place in those villages which belong to the Medak district. There is a proposal by APIIC to acquire about 1,300 acres in Pashamailaram and another extent of 1,500 acres in Sangareddy *taluk* abutting Sangareddy, Tamailkhanpet and Rudraram road for the needs of industry and housing. Through this kind of industrial development policy, there is likely to be a linear industrial growth along the highway alone. Instead of spending investment only along highway, it would be better to concentrate the industrial development at Sangareddy town. This would avoid high costs on infrastructure and social services and housing facilities. The development of industries, five miles away from Patancheruvu will create population pressure on Ramachandrapuram-Patancheruvu because of the available service facilities.

TABLE 10.1 : Standards for Shopping Facilities Recommended by TCPO for Industrial Townships

Sl. No.	*Unit*	*Hierarchy of shopping centre*	*No. of shops per 1000 population*	*Average area sq.ft. per shop*	*Total area allocated for shopping centre*
1.	Neighbourhood (pop. 4,000	Convenience shop corner shops	3 + 1 mobile shop	100	0.1 acre
2.	Sector (pop. 12,000)	Local shopping Centre		150	1.25-1.50 acres
3.	District (pop. 35,000-40,000)	Community shopping	4-5 + 2 mobile shops 3.00 - 3.50	200	3.50-4.00 acres
4.	Town (pop. 30,000)	Central shopping	2.00-2.50 + 0.5 mobile shops	300	35 to 40 acres

Source: B.S. Bhoosan & K.V. Sundaram (1976). *Quality of Life in Human Settlements*, Institute of Development Studies.

At present APIIC does not have any large-scale industrial development proposal in the area, but the established industries may lead to the birth of some more industries. It should be seen that these industries do not occupy the land which could be used for productive agricultural purposes as pointed out earlier.

Development of Transportation Network

Before any major proposal on housing and community services, there is a need to improve the existing transportation network. There are two proposed ring roads of HUDA passing through Ramachandrapuram-Patancheruvu zone. One is the outer ring road passing through

Patancheruvu, Pocharam and Muthangi, and the other is intermediate ring road as shown in the Map 10.1.

At present the villages are linked with cart-tracks or unmetalled roads. Using the present road accessability, all the village sites should be connected efficiently to use as principal traffic routes or major roads. The width of these major roads may range from 80′ to 100′ as per the recommended standards for industrial townships by Town and Country Planning Organisation (TCPO).

Housing and Community Facilities

The policy to develop industries in the villages of Medak leaves the option for bulk of housing in those villages located in Rangareddy district. Thus, the future housing development is likely to take place in Patancheruvu, Ramachandrapuram, Chandanagar, Nalagandla, Tellapur, Gopanpalli, Serilingampalli, Madeenaguda, Hafeezpet, Kondapur, Kothaguda and Gachibowli.

The important organisations likely to be involved in the housing development are Hyderabad Urban Development Authority, APIIC, Co-operative societies, Industrial worker unions and private individuals. Before indulging in any large-scale housing development there is a need to have a basic framework on which these different housing organisations could work.

At present the entire area is pre-dominantly an agricultural tract except the BHEL township and some housing development in and around Taranagar and Patancheruvu. The built up area is largely rural in character and most of the land is either put to agriculture or laying barren.

There is a need to know the existing size of population before indulging in any framework for housing development. Previously the population was projected on the basis of growth rate between 1961 and 1971, and it is not always true that the same growth rate continued between 1971 and 1981. Another reasonable way of projecting the population is based on the proportion of employment and population. The activity rate is the ratio of population to total employment.

Activity rate in 1971 = total population/total employment
= 38,103/13800 = 2.76

MAP 10.1 : Ramachandrapuram-Patancheruvu Zone — Proposal Map

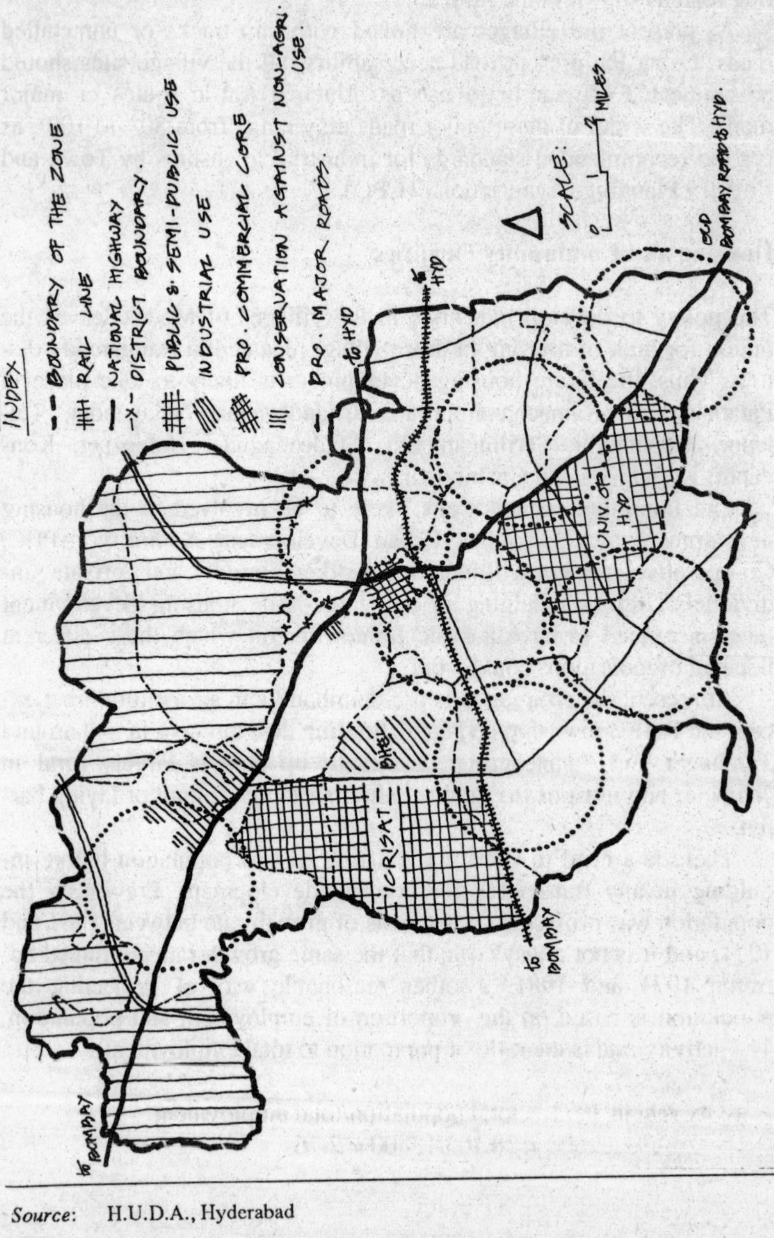

Source: H.U.D.A., Hyderabad

Now to find the 1981 population in the area, the bulk of the employment is through the establishment of various industries around Ramachandrapuram-Patancheruvu after 1971.

Total industrial employment in these industries = 4,180
(includes large, medium and small-scale industries)

Adding this industrial employment to the total employment in 1971 it comes to 17,984. Assuming the same activity rate of 2.76 till 1981, then the population could be calculated as follows :

Total employment x activity rate in 1981

$17{,}984 \times 2.76 = 49{,}636$

Thus, the total population in 1981 is 49,636 excluding the service population.

The existing service facilities are limited to the village requirements with some concentration of educational and health facilities at Patancheruvu and BHEL town. This area is likely to put up the urban characteristics suddenly with large-scale housing and acquisition of agriculture and other land. There is no need to exaggerate that the present infrastructure and social service facilities are not adequate to meet the future population needs. So there is a need to organise the new development on a fresh ground in an integrated manner without causing harm to the existing population.

To create a broad framework for the future development of housing and service facilities there is a need to identify central places. The central places are identified with the concentration of activities because they largely develop on the basis of threshold population and accessability. The urban geographers give enough emphasis on the hierarchy of shopping centres to study the relation between form and functions of the town. W. Burns published a book suggesting four-tier hierarchy of shopping centres.

1. The Town Centre,
2. District Centre,
3. Neighbourhood Centre,
4. Sub-Centre.

This is a broad-based framework suggested by him depending on the consumer convenience and frequency of visits. His argument further leads to some polishing but the basic framework of nesting arrangement is useful.

Almost on a similar line, the TCPO suggested the following four-tier system of hierarchy of shopping centres for industrial townships :

	Threshold	*Accessability*
At Town level	300,000	—
At District level	35,000-40,000	—
At Sector level	12,000	(mile (1.61 km)
At Neighbourhood level	4,000	$^1/_4$ to $^1/_2$ mile (0.40 to 0.80 km)

Applying the above hierarchy of shopping centres to the case of Ramachandrapuram-Patanacheruvu zone, the identified town centre is at Taranagar due to its centrality function of trade and commerce. There should be an intermediate level centrality to combine the town centre with the surrounding development.

To get that intermediate level of shopping centre, the shopping at sectoral level of 12,000 could be a viable unit. The existing village sites can be taken as focal points and the maximum accessability is one mile from this centre. Thus the shopping centres at sectoral level could be developed at Patancheruvu, Chandanagar, Nalagandla, Tellapur, Gopanpalli, Kondapur and Gachibowli village sites. Three such sectors should support a community shopping centre.

As per the standards each sector can support a population of 12,000 and this need not be uniform for all the sectors because the sectors near the core should be developed with higher densities. There are three sectors around the core which should be developed with higher residential densities including Patancheruvu.

Density	*Gross density*
Low	30 persons/acre
Medium	40-50 persons/acre
High	60-70 person/acre
Intensive	100-150 persons/acre

The residential density standards prescribed in the Development Plan of Hyderabad are more useful than adopting the general planning standards. The Development of Hyderabad prescribes the following residential densities for Hyderabad city.

If the high residential densities are adopted in the above-mentioned villages around the core it will lead to a compact development than adopting low densities and spending high infrastructure costs.

BIBLIOGRAPHY

Alam Manzoor (1969). "The Hyderabad Metropolitan Research Project", prepared by Osmania University & Institute of Asian Studies, Hyderbad.

Alam Manzoor and Khan Waheeduddin (1972). *Matropolitan Hyderabad and its region*, Asia Publishing House, Madras.

Boskoff Alvin (1982). *The Sociology of Urban Regions*, Mereditt Publishing Company, New York.

Cardon Carol (1977). *Planned Cities*, Sage Publications, London.

Catanese J. Anthoney & Snyder C. James (1979). *Introduction to Urban Planning* McGraw-Hill Book Company, New York.

Cherry & Gordon (1970). *Town Planning in its Social Context*, Leonard Hill, London.

Cherry & Gordon (1974). *Urban Planning Problems*, Leonard & Hill, London.

Claire H.W.M. (1960). *Handbook on Urban Planning*, Van Nostrand Reinhold Company, New York, Toronto, London.

Clapp A. James (1971). *New Towns and Urban Regions*, Mereditt Publishing Company, New York.

Dickinson E. Robert (1960). *City Region and Regionalism : A Geographical Contribution to Regionalism*, Routledge and Kegan Paul Ltd., London.

Doxiadix C.A. (1977). *The Human Settlements that we need*, Tata-McGraw-Hill Publishing Company Ltd., New Delhi.

Epstein G. David (1973). *Brasilia-Plan and Reality*, University of California Press, Los Angeles.

Fishman robert (1977). *Urban Utopias in the Twentieth Century*, Basic Book inc., Publishers, New York.

Foley L. Donald (1972). *Governing the London Region : Re-organisation and Planning in the 1960's* Institute of Govt. Studies, University of California Press, Berkley.

Geddes Patrick (1949). *Cities in Evolution*, William & Norgate Ltd., London.

Gibbs J.P. (1961). *Urban Research methods*, D. Vand Mostr & Co.

Gilson J.E. (1977). *Designing the new city : A Systematic Approach*, John Wiley and Sons, London.

Hertzen Von & Spreiregan D. (1971). *Building a New Town : Tapiola-Finland's New Garden City*, The MIT Press, Cambridge. Massachusetts.

Hicks K. Ursula (1974). *Large City*, The Macmillan Press Ltd., London.

Hyderabad Urban Development Authority (1975). Development Plan for the area comprising the Municipal Corporation of Hyderabad.

Jakobson Leo & Prakash Ved (1974). *Metropolitan Growth*, Halsted Press Division, John Wiley & Sons, New York. London. Sydney. Toronto.

Jensen Relf (1974). *Cities of Vision*, Applied Science Publishers Ltd., London.

Mahadev P.D. (1975). *People, Space and Economy of an Indian City*, Institute of Development Studies, Mysore.

McLoughlin Brain J. (1973). *Control and Urban Planning*, Faber & Faber Ltd., London.

Mellor J.R. (1977). *Urban Sociology in an Urbanised Society*, Routledge and Kegan Paul, London.

Misra R.P. (1978). *Million Cities in India*, Vikas Publishing House Pvt. Ltd., New Delhi, Bombay, Bangalore, Calcutta, Kanpur.

Muthayya B.C. & Mathur T.S. (1975). *Rehabilitation of Displaced Villagers*, National Institute of Cummunity Development, Hyderabad.

Noble G. & Dutta K. (1977). *Indian Urbanisation and Planning*, Tata McGraw-Hill Publishing Company Ltd., New Delhi.

Schnore F. Leo (1965). *The Urban Scene*, Collier-Macmillan Ltd., London.

Sivaramakrishnan K.C. (1978). *Indian Urban Scene*, Indian Institute of Advanced Study, Simla.

Solesbury William (1979). *Policy in Urban Planning*, Peragamon Press, Oxford.

Spreiregan D. Paul (1971). *The Modern Metropolis*, The MIT Press, Cambridge. Massachusetts, London.

Town and Country Planning Organisation: " National Capital Region", (Memeographed). New Delhi.

Turner Roy (1962). *India's Urban Future*, Oxford University Press. Bombay.

Van Cleef Eugene (1970). *Cities in Action*, Peragamon Press, New York. Toronto. Oxford.

Woodbury Coleman (1953). *The Future of Cities and Urban Re-development : Sociological Study*, The University of Chicago Press.

Index